IELTS

Practice Tests 1

with answers

James Milton-Huw Bell-Petre Neville

Express Publishing

Published by Express Publishing

Liberty House, New Greenham Park, Newbury, Berkshire RG19 6HW
Tel: (0044) 1635 817 363 - Fax: (0044) 1635 817 463
e-mail: inquiries@expresspublishing.co.uk
http://www.expresspublishing.co.uk

First published 2002

ISBN 1-84216-751-0

CONTENTS

INTRODUCTION TO IELTS

IELTS is a testing system which assesses how good a person's English language is for the purpose of study or training. The test is recognised around the world by universities and colleges.

There are two forms to the test:

Academic: which tests a person's language for university study
General Training: which tests basic survival skills with education or immigration in mind

There are 4 parts to each test. The Listening and Speaking tests are the same for both Academic and General Training forms of the test. There are separate papers for the Reading and Writing tests. The organisation looks like this:

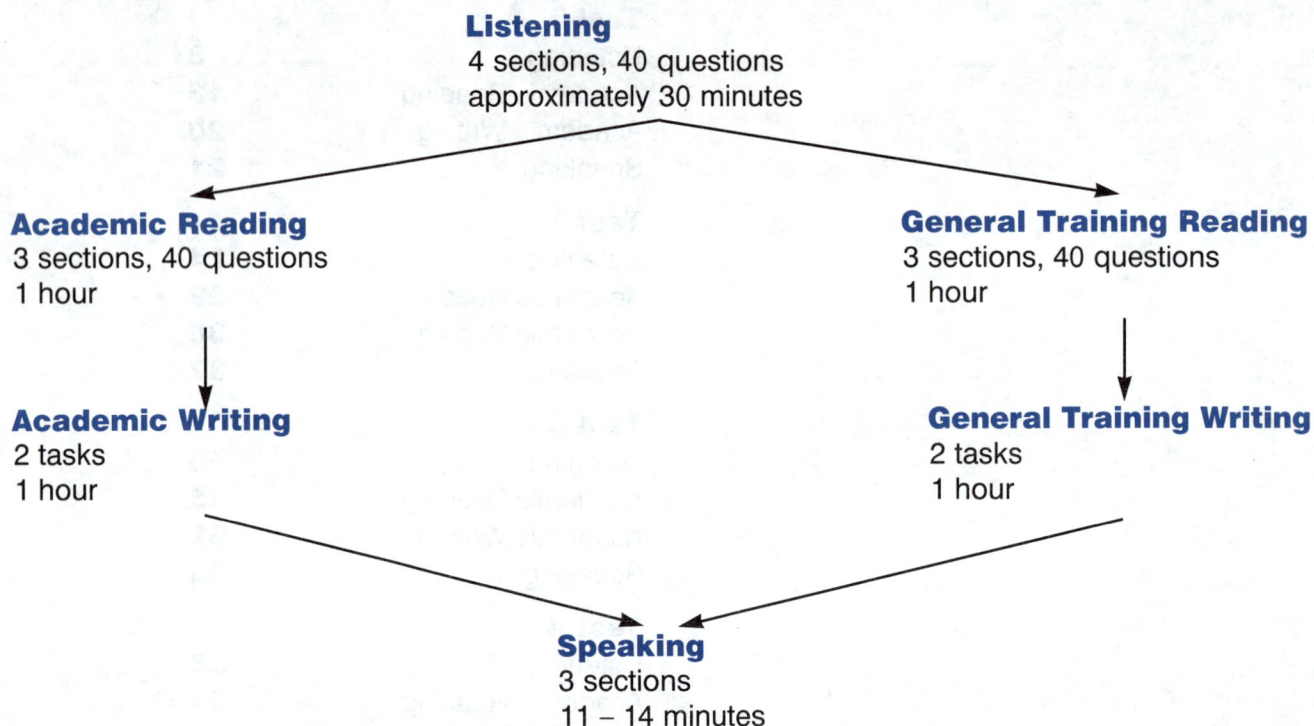

Listening
4 sections, 40 questions
approximately 30 minutes

Academic Reading
3 sections, 40 questions
1 hour

General Training Reading
3 sections, 40 questions
1 hour

Academic Writing
2 tasks
1 hour

General Training Writing
2 tasks
1 hour

Speaking
3 sections
11 – 14 minutes

This book contains practice tests to help prepare students for these tests whichever form of the test they take. Choose the Reading and Writing tasks appropriate for the exam being taken.

HOW IS IELTS ASSESSED?

You will receive a general assessment of 0 – 9 based on the average of the individual scores from each of the four components. All four sections of the test are equally weighted. The Listening and Reading sections are marked in half and whole points whereas the Speaking and Writing components are graded only as whole points.

An overview of the nine bands is written below to help you understand the level of the band you have to gain to be accepted on your course.

9 Expert User: native speaker level. Can function appropriately and accurately in all skills.

8 Very Good User: has excellent command of the language but may produce some errors in unfamiliar circumstances.

7 Good User: generally handles language well but with some inaccuracies. Can produce a competent written argument. Can understand abstract reasoning in reading passages.

6 Competent User: has reasonable control of the language but with some inaccuracies. May have some difficulties with unfamiliar situations.

5 Modest User: can deal adequately with language in his own area but will find difficulty in dealing with complex language and unfamiliar situations.

4 Limited User: only able to deal with familiar situations and not complex language. Often has difficulty in understanding and expression.

3 Very Limited User: has problems in communicating. Able to express general meaning only in familiar circumstances.

2 Intermittent User: has many difficulties using the language. Can only communicate very little basic information by using a few words or phrases.

1 Non User: has no ability to communicate except for a few isolated words.

0 Did not write the test: did not produce any information to be assessed.

How to understand the scores

When each component has been marked, a raw score is given and this is then converted into an equivalent IELTS grade. The raw scores and their IELTS equivalents are given below.

There is no official pass mark and the grade the candidate is required to attain depends on the subject to be studied or the institution e.g. Science and Engineering departments ask for lower scores than Law and Literature.

It is usual for a university to ask for a minimum of IELTS 6 as the basic entry requirement and the average score is normally what is looked at. However, if the course you have chosen consists of mostly reading and writing, if you get 5 in either of these disciplines, then you may not be accepted even if your overall score is 7. Each institution will set out its own criteria for the individual candidate.

When you do the tests you should aim for a minimum score of 24/25 in both the Reading and Listening components before entering for the IELTS examination. If you do not manage to get the score you require for your course, you will have to wait three months before you are allowed to resit the IELTS test. It is better to be sure of passing the IELTS successfully the first time you enter yourself rather than using it as a practice run.

Reading		Listening	
IELTS	RAW	IELTS	RAW
1	1	1	1
2	2, 3	2	2, 3
3	4, 5, 6, 7	3	4, 5, 6
3.5	8, 9, 10	3.5	7, 8, 9
4	11, 12, 13	4	10, 11, 12
4.5	14,1 5, 16	4.5	13, 14,1 5, 16
5	17, 18, 19	5	17, 18, 19, 20
5.5	20, 21, 22, 23,	5.5	21, 22, 23, 24
6	24, 25, 26, 27	6	25, 26, 27, 28
6.5	28, 29, 30	6.5	29, 30, 31
7	31, 32, 33	7	32, 33
7.5	34, 35	7.5	34, 35
8	36, 37,	8	36, 37
8.5	38, 39	8.5	38, 39
9	40	9	40

Tips for IELTS students

The following is some advice and information to help candidates sitting for the exam.

General Information

a In the IELTS there are no half marks for each question in the Listening and Reading papers.

b Spelling correctly is important. Both British and American English spelling is accepted but be consistent and do not mix styles.

c If you are not sure of an answer, do not write two possible choices. Even if one is correct, you will not be credited with a mark.

d Always read the instructions carefully before you start an exercise as they can vary in IELTS.

Listening

a Don't lose your concentration and pay close attention to the cassette as you only hear each passage once.

b Do not spend too long on a difficult question as you may miss the necessary information you need for the next few questions. Instead, mark the number of the question you are having problems with and look at it again during the copying up time.

c Always use the 10 minutes given at the end of the test to check your work and not merely to copy your answers onto the computer sheet.

d Make sure you fill in the answers in the correct box on the computer sheet.

e Always be aware that there will be distractors to the questions given in the texts so do not simply write the first possible answer you hear. That answer may be contradicted a little later.

f Make sure you are familiar with the alphabet as some answers require you to note down the spelling of a word.

g Accustom yourself to listening to different accents. You will hear a variety of accents on the cassette but British or Australian are the most common.

Reading

a Always read the instructions to the tasks as they may vary from test to test.

b Make sure you complete the computer sheet after each reading. You are **not** given any extra time at the end of the test to fill in the sheet.

c Do not spend more than 20 minutes on each section as you may not have enough time to complete the three passages. Always time yourself when doing the practice tests to get used to finishing each section in 20 minutes.

d As the sections of the Reading test become progressively more difficult, if you take longer than 20 minutes on the first two sections, you will have little chance of finishing the third passage.

e As the IELTS Reading paper covers a variety of written styles, make sure you prepare yourself for this by reading newspapers, journals, magazines and fiction and non-fiction books.

f Be prepared to be tested on any subject someone attending a university would be expected to be aware of. However, you are not expected to be an expert in all these topics.

g Sometimes in IELTS the questions are written before as well as after the passage. Always check that you have answered 40 questions.

Writing

a Always make sure you fully understand the question and write a plan before you start your essay. In Task One, interpreting the information in the table correctly is one factor which influences the final Writing mark.

b Be aware of time and never be tempted to spend more than 20 minutes on Task One at the expense of Task Two which has a higher weighting.

c Always leave some time to check your essays.

d Always write the minimum number of words given as short essays will be penalised. There is no maximum number of words for each essay.

Speaking

a Many questions in Part One concerning your personal life can be predicted and prepared before the interview. However, do not learn set answers by heart as the examiner will recognise this. You will be tested on your ability to speak English fluently and naturally so think about the possible questions and make some notes on what replies you could give rather than writing speeches.

b Do not search for a particular word for very long. Instead resort to paraphrasing.

c If you don't understand a question, do not be afraid to ask the examiner to repeat or rephrase it. If you are unsure and misinterpret the question, then you will not give an appropriate reply.

d There are no right or wrong answers to the tasks. You will be tested on your ability to discuss a topic effectively in English with a native speaker and not on your general knowledge.

PRACTICE
TEST 1

LISTENING
PRACTICE TEST 1

NUMBER OF QUESTIONS: 40
APPROX. TIME: 30 MINUTES

Instructions

You will hear a number of conversations and talks and you must answer all the questions you hear. The conversations are recorded and you will have time to read the instructions and questions, and to check your work.

The tape will be played only ONCE.

The test is organised in 4 sections.

You can write your answers on the question paper and at the end of the test you will be given time to transfer your answers to an answer sheet.

Section 1 | Questions 1 - 10

Questions 1 - 3

Circle the correct answer.

Example

Sergeant Brown is going to speak about
A   comfort.
(B) safety.
C   the police.
D   Mr Fogerty.

---

1   Sergeant Brown is
   A   the community patrol officer.
   B   the university security officer.
   C   the community police adviser.
   D   the university liaison officer.

2   Sergeant Brown
   A   lives locally and is not married.
   B   lives on the campus and has two daughters.
   C   has a son at the university.
   D   doesn't live on the campus with his daughters.

3   Sergeant Brown has been a police officer for
   A   5 years.
   B   10 years.
   C   15 years.
   D   20 years.

Questions 4 - 6

*Write **NO MORE THAN THREE WORDS** for each answer.*

4   The most dangerous place around the campus is ....
5   The most dangerous place in town is ....
6   It is dangerous because of ....

Questions 7 - 8

*Circle **TWO** answers **A-E**.*

Which TWO items should a student always carry?
   A   a personal alarm
   B   valuables
   C   their passport
   D   jewellery
   E   some identification

9

Questions 9 - 10
Circle TWO letters A - E.

Which TWO things does Sergeant Brown recommend a student should do?
 A walk home in pairs
 B use public transport
 C drive home
 D arrange to be home at a certain time
 E not carry a lot of cash

Section 2 Questions 11 - 20

Questions 11 - 13
Circle THREE letters A - E.

What are John and Sarah discussing?
 A the amount of work in the second year
 B the importance of medieval history
 C studying material in a different language
 D when their exams will finish
 E the level of work in the second year

Questions 14 and 15
Write NO MORE THAN THREE WORDS for each answer.

14 Why is Sarah working in the market?
....

15 How many courses must John and Sarah choose?
....

Questions 16 - 20
Write A NUMBER or NO MORE THAN THREE WORDS for each space.

Course	Credits	Tutor	Recommended reading	Requirements
Medieval Society	20	Dr Smith	Study pack	.... (17)
Development of Technology	20	Mr Mills	Bouchier's '... ....' (18)	None
The Crusades I	10	.... (19)	Allison & McKay's 'The First Crusades'	French
The Crusades II	10	Dr Shaker & Professor Lord	Mallen's 'A General History of the Crusades'	French
Peasants and Kings	.... (16)	Dr Reeves	Hobart's 'Introduction to the Middle Ages'	.... (20)

Section 3 | Questions 21 - 30

Questions 21 - 25

*Circle the correct letters **A - C**.*

21 Dr Mullet was particularly impressed by Fayed's
  A final year dissertation.
  B application form.
  C exam results.

22 After he took his exams, Fayed felt
  A nervous.
  B anxious.
  C happy.

23 Dr Mullet accepts people for the MA course because of
  A their exam results.
  B their ability to play games.
  C a variety of reasons.

24 What did Fayed initially go to university to study?
  A economics.
  B booms and crashes.
  C history.

25 The course Fayed is applying for is concerned with
  A the developing world.
  B the development of banks.
  C the economics of work.

Questions 26 - 30

*Complete Dr Mullet's notes on his interview with Fayed in **NO MORE THAN THREE WORDS** for each space.*

INTERVIEW WITH FAYED

Worried! Far from his country. .... (26)?

Will go to study in .... (27)
if not accepted here.

After university wants to work .... (28).

Now going to visit .... (29).

My decision – when? .... (30)

Section 4 Questions 31 - 40

Questions 31 - 35

Complete each sentence with NO MORE THAN THREE WORDS.

31 The public has more knowledge of vitamins than other parts ....

32 The public doesn't always eat ....

33 There is a widespread belief that Vitamin C can ....

34 Vitamin A helps you see ....

35 Many people wrongly think that taking vitamin supplements can ....

Questions 34 - 40

Complete each space with NO MORE THAN THREE WORDS or A NUMBER.

Vitamin	Name	Helps the body	Daily need	Where to get it
A	Retinol	have good vision, ... (36) infection	750 mg	liver, butter, egg yolks, milk
D	Calciferol	form healthy bones and .... (37)	varies with age	sunlight, cod liver oil
E	Tocopherol	control fat	.... (38) mg	wheatgerm, oils, eggs, butter
K		coagulate blood	varies	green vegetables, liver, eggs
B complex		metabolise carbohydrates form healthy tissue and .... (39)	varies	yeast, cereals, milk, cheese, offal
C	Ascorbic acid	fight infection, fight scurvy	30 mg	.... (40)

ACADEMIC READING
PRACTICE TEST 1

NUMBER OF QUESTIONS: 40

TIME PERMITTED: 1 HOUR

Instructions

WRITE ALL ANSWERS ON THE ANSWER SHEET

The test is organised as follows:

Reading Passage 1	Questions 1 - 15
Reading Passage 2	Questions 16 - 27
Reading Passage 3	Questions 28 - 40

Start at the beginning of the test and read the passages in order. Answer all the questions. If you are not sure of an answer, you can leave it and try to answer it later.

Section 1

*You should spend about 20 minutes on questions **1 - 15**, which are based on Reading Passage 1 below.*

National **Parks** and Climate **Change**

A National parks, nature reserves, protected areas and sites of special scientific interest (SSSIs) are an important part of the natural landscape in most countries. Their habitat and terrains vary massively from tundra and glacier parks in the north to wetlands in Europe, steppes in central and eastern Europe, and prairie grasslands and deserts in other areas. Virtually all kinds of landscape are protected somewhere. And these protected areas are important for the variety of plant and animal life they harbour: caribou, bears, wolves, rare types of fish and birds.

B But these areas are under threat from a recent peril – global climate change. No amount of legislation in any one country can protect against a worldwide problem. What exactly are the problems caused by climate change? David Woodward, head of the British Council for Nature Conservation, spoke to 'Science Now' about some of these areas, and his first point highlighted the enormous variation in nature reserves.

C "Each park or reserve is an ecosystem," he says, "and the larger reserves, such as those in Canada, may have several types of ecological subsystems within it. There are reserves which are half the size of Western Europe, so it doesn't make sense to talk about them as if they were all the same, or as if the microclimates within them were uniform." Woodward outlines some of the dangers posed by climatic change to parks in the northern Americas, for example.

D "If climatic change is severe, and in particular if the change is happening as quickly as it is at the moment, then the boundaries of the park no longer make much sense. A park that was designated as a protected area 90 years ago may suffer such change in its climate that the nature of it changes too. It will no longer contain the animal and plant life that it did. So the area which once protected, say, a species of reindeer or a type of scenery, will have changed. In effect, you lose the thing you were trying to protect." This effect has already been seen in Canada, where parks which once contained glaciers have seen the glaciers melted by global warming.

E Jennie Lindstrom, Chief Executive Officer of H_2O, the charity which campaigns on an international level on behalf of mainland Europe's protected wetland and wilderness areas, is even more pessimistic. In a letter to Science Now, she has asserted that up to 70% of such areas are already experiencing such "significant change ... in climate" that the distribution patterns of flora and fauna are changing, and that all areas will eventually be affected. She estimates that the most profound change is occurring in the northernmost parks in areas such as Finland, Greenland, Iceland and northern Russia, but adds that "there is no place which will not suffer the effects of global warming. What we are seeing is a massive change in the environment – and that means the extinction of whole species, as well as visual and structural changes which means that areas like the Camargue may literally look totally different in 50 or 60 years' time."

F The problems are manifold. First, it is difficult or impossible to predict which areas are most in need of help – that is, which areas are in most danger. Predicting climate change is even more unreliable than predicting the weather. Secondly, there is a sense that governments in most areas are apathetic towards a problem which may not manifest itself until long after that government's term of office has come to an end. In poor areas, of course, nature conservation is low on the list of priorities compared to, say, employment or health. Third, and perhaps most important, even in areas where there is both the political will and the financial muscle to do something about the problem, it is hard to know just what to do. Maria Colehill of Forestlife, an American conservation body, thinks that in the case of climate change, the most we can realistically do is monitor the situation and allow for the changes that we cannot prevent, while lobbying governments internationally to make the changes to the pollution laws, for example, that will enable us to deal with the causes of the problem. "I am despondent," she admits. "I have no doubt that a lot of the work we are doing on behalf of the North American lynx, for example, will be wasted. The animal itself can live in virtually any environment where there are few humans, but of course its numbers are small. If climate change affects the other animal life in the areas where it now lives, if the food chain changes, then the lynx will be affected too. Less food for the lynx means fewer lynxes, or lynxes with nowhere to go."

G Certainly, climate change is not going to go away overnight. It is estimated that fossil fuels burnt in the 1950s will still be affecting our climate in another 30 years, so the changes will continue for some time after that. If we want to protect the remnants of our wild landscapes for future generations, the impetus for change must come from the governments of the world.

Questions 1 - 7

*Do the following statements agree with the information given in Reading Passage 1? In boxes 1 - 7 on your answer sheet write **Yes** if the statement agrees with the information, **No** if the statement contradicts the information, **Not Given** if there is no information on this in the passage.*

1 Every country has protected areas or national parks. Yes
2 Countries can protect their parks by changing their laws. No
3 A protected area or park can contain many different ecosystems. YES
4 David Woodward thinks that Canadian parks will all be different in 90 years. YES
5 Canada, more than any other country, has felt the effects of global warming. NOT GIVEN
6 H_2O works to protect wetlands everywhere. YES
7 Some parts of the world will feel the results of global warming more than others. YES

Questions 8 - 13

Complete the summary below. Choose your answers from the box below the summary and write them in boxes 8 - 13 on the answer sheet. There are more words than spaces, so you will not use all the given words.

There are ...many problems... (8) in attempting to stop the effects of ...global warming... (9). One is the problem of predicting change. Another is a lack of ...governmental willingness... (10) to change the situation; most governments' interest in the problem is limited because the problem will not become very serious ...internationally... (11). Finally, there is the problem of what action we should actually take. One solution is both to keep an eye on the situation as it develops, and to push for changes ...locally... (12). Even if we do this, the problem is not going to ...go away overnight... (13), since it takes a considerable time for global warming to happen.

governmental willingness	lots of ways	global warming
internationally	for many years	locally
go away overnight	many problems	after all

Questions 14 and 15

Reading Passage 1 has seven paragraphs A - G. Which paragraphs state the following information? Write the appropriate letters A - G in boxes 14 and 15 on your answer sheet.

14 All areas of the world are likely to be affected by global climate changes.

15 Remedies for global warming will not reverse these trends immediately.

Section 2

*You should spend about 20 minutes on questions **16 - 27**, which are based on Reading Passage 2 below.*

The Truth About *art*

Modern art has had something of a bad press recently – or, to be more precise; it has always had a bad press in certain newspapers and amongst certain sectors of the public. In the public mind, it seems, art (that is, graphic art – pictures – and spatial art – sculpture) is divided into two broad categories. The first is "classic" art, by which is meant representational painting, drawing and sculpture; the second is "modern" art, also known as "abstract" or "non-representational". British popular taste runs decidedly in favour of the former, if one believes a recent survey conducted by Sir Bruce McGowen, owner of the Tarn Gallery and Workshops in Suffolk, and one of Britain's most influential artistic commentators. He found that the "man (or woman) in the street" has a distrust of cubism, abstracts, sculptures made of bricks and all types of so-called "found" art. He likes Turner and Constable, the great representatives of British watercolour and oil painting respectively, or the French Impressionists, and his taste for statues is limited to the realistic figures of the great and good that litter the British landscape – Robin Hood in Nottingham and Oliver Cromwell outside the Houses of Parliament. This everyman does not believe in primary colours, abstraction and geometry in nature – the most common comment is that such-and-such a painting is "something a child could have done".

Maurice Coates, director of the Buckinghamshire Galleries in Windsor, which specialises in modern painting, agrees. "Look around you at what 'art' is available every day," he says. "Our great museums and galleries specialise in work which is designed to appeal to the lowest common denominator. It may be representational, it may be 'realistic' in one sense, but a lot of it wouldn't make it into the great European galleries. Britain has had maybe two or three major world painters in the last 1000 years, so we make up the space with a lot of second-rate material."

Coates believes that our ignorance of what "modern art" is has been caused by this lack of exposure to truly great art. He compares the experience of the average British city-dweller with that of a citizen of Italy, France or Spain.

"Of course, we don't appreciate any kind of art in the same way because of the paucity of good art in Britain. We don't have galleries of the quality of those in Madrid, Paris, Versailles, Florence, New York or even some places in Russia. We distrust good art – by which I mean both modern and traditional artistic

forms – because we don't have enough of it to learn about it. In other countries, people are surrounded by it from birth. Indeed they take it as a birthright, and are proud of it. The British tend to be suspicious of it. It's not valued here."

Not all agree. Jane Forrester, who runs the Hampshire Art House, believes that while the British do not have the same history of artistic experience as many European countries, their senses are as finely attuned to art as anyone else's.

"Look at what sells – in the great art auction houses, in greetings cards, in posters. Look at what's going on in local amateur art classes up and down the country. Of course, the British are not the same as other countries, but that's true of all nationalities. The French artistic experience and outlook is not the same as the Italian. In Britain, we have artistic influences from all over the world. There's the Irish, Welsh, and Scottish influences, as well as Caribbean, African and European. We also have strong links with the Far East, in particular the Indian subcontinent. All these influences come to bear in creating a British artistic outlook. There's this tendency to say that British people only want garish pictures of clowns crying or ships sailing into battle, and that anything new or different is misunderstood. That's not my experience at all. The British public is poorly educated in art, but that's not the same as being uninterested in it."

Forrester points to Britain's long tradition of visionary artists such as William Blake, the London engraver and poet who died in 1827. Artists like Blake tended to be one-offs rather than members of a school, and their work is diverse and often word-based so it is difficult to export.

Perhaps, as ever, the truth is somewhere in between these two opinions. It is true that visits to traditional galleries like the National and the National Portrait Gallery outnumber attendance at more modern shows, but this is the case in every country except Spain, perhaps because of the influence of the two most famous non-traditional Spanish painters of the 20th century, Picasso and Dali. However, what is also true is that Britain has produced a long line of individual artists with unique, almost unclassifiable styles such as Blake, Samuel Palmer and Henry Moore.

Questions 16 - 24

Classify the following statements as referring to

    A   Sir Bruce McGowen

    B   Maurice Coates

    C   Jane Forrester

    D   None of the above

*Write the appropriate letters **A - D** in boxes 16 - 24 on your answer sheet.*

16   British people don't appreciate art because they don't see enough art around them all the time.

17   British museums aim to appeal to popular tastes in art.

18   The average Englishman likes the works of Turner and Constable.

19   Britain, like every other country, has its own view of what art is.

20   In Britain, interest in art is mainly limited to traditional forms such as representational painting.

21   Art in France and Italy has been affected by other cultures.

22   Galleries in other countries are of better quality than those in Britain.

23   People are not raised to appreciate art.

24   The British have a limited knowledge of art.

Questions 25 - 27

*For questions 25 - 27, choose the best answers, **A, B, C** or **D**, according to the information in the text. Write your answers in boxes 25 - 27 on your answer sheet.*

25 Many British artists

    A   are engravers or poets.

    B   are great but liked only in Britain.

    C   do not belong to a school or general trend.

    D   are influenced by Picasso and Dali.

26 "Classic" art can be described as

    A   sentimental, realistic paintings with geometric shapes.

    B   realistic paintings with primary colours.

    C   abstract modern paintings and sculptures.

    D   realistic, representational pictures and sculptures.

27 In Spain people probably enjoy modern art because

    A   their artists have a classifiable style.

    B   the most renowned modern artists are Spanish.

    C   they attend many modern exhibitions.

    D   they have different opinions on art.

Section 3

You should spend about 20 minutes on questions 28 - 40, which are based on Reading Passage 3 below.

Australian Aborigines Demand Return of Remains

As a former British colony, Australia has close cultural and historical links with the United Kingdom, due to the British and Irish settlers who arrived in droves in the 19th and 20th centuries. One aspect of this contact is the role of Britain, and British archeologists and collectors, in taking Aboriginal bones, relics and artifacts from Australia to museums and collections in the UK. Now leaders of the indigenous people of Australia, the Aborigines, are demanding that any aboriginal remains in the UK are returned to Australia.

In 19th century Britain, there was a mania for collecting all kinds of objects from other countries. These were sent home, where they were kept in museums such as the British Museum and the Natural History Museum. Museums in the UK have a huge number of such objects – objects which, say protesters, were basically stolen during Britain's long colonial history, with little or no regard for the feelings or rights of the people to whom the objects originally belonged.

Now the Australian Prime Minister is supporting Aboriginal calls for the objects and remains to be returned to their original home. A spokesman for the Aboriginal Council of New South Wales, Stevie McCoy, said: " The bones do not belong abroad. They belong here. This is about beliefs, and a traditional Aboriginal belief is that our ancestors can only find peace if their remains are buried in the homeland."

There are certainly lots of Aboriginal remains in the UK, although their exact locations are not entirely clear. What is known is that, between them, the British Museum and the Natural History Museum have some 2000-2500 artifacts composed of human remains, although the museums point out that only about 500 of these are of Aboriginal origin. Dr William Cowell Bell, for the London Museum Association, adds that "A lot of the objects are not human remains in their original form, but are made out of human remains. These include decorated skulls and bones from which charms and amulets have been created." A smaller number of similar artifacts are known to be held in collections in Oxford and Cambridge.

There is some sensitivity to Aboriginal demands in the archeological world. Lady Amanda Spurway, life president of the Glover Museum in London, says that the museum has had its small collection of Aboriginal remains packed ready for return for a decade, and is only waiting for information about where they must go.

The National College of Surgeons says it will return the remains of any individual who can be named (although it is obviously difficult to put names to them after such a long time). This growing sensitivity to the hitherto ignored rights of indigenous peoples around the world has caused some relics to be restored to their original country, particularly in Scotland, where a group of Aboriginal remains has already been returned. Edinburgh University has returned skulls and bones to Tasmania and New Zealand.

One problem, according to legal expert Ewan Mather, is that the law allowing museums to decide what to do with these objects is more relaxed in Scotland. English museums, on the other hand, are not allowed (either by law or by the groups of trustees who run them) to just hand back remains of their own accord. However, British supporters of the Aborigines claim that such restrictive laws are inhumane in the modern world, and that it would be a simple enough matter to change them in order to allow the items to be returned.

A further objection to handing back relics is because of their scientific value claim some museum directors. Dr Bell believes that the size of the collection in the Natural History Museum in Lincoln made it a very valuable resource in the analysis of the way of life of Aborigines, and could be used to study the origin and development of the people. Breaking up the collection might mean that such knowledge could be lost forever.

Aboriginal groups, however, respond by pointing out that the scientific importance of the remains has to be seen against a backdrop of human rights. "I doubt whether the British government would allow several thousand bones of British soldiers to be used for 'scientific purposes' in any other country," said Stevie McCoy, with a hint of irony. "Would the families allow it? I think there would be a public outcry, no matter how old the remains were. This practice [of taking bones and human remains] went on from the first moment the white man came to Australia right up to the early part of the 20th century. It is a scandal."

The British government, meanwhile, has announced that it will set up a working party to discuss the possibility of changes to the law. This might allow museums to negotiate on their own with Aboriginal and other groups around the world.

Questions 28 - 30

*Choose the **two** best answers according to the text, and write the letters **A - E** in boxes 28 - 30 on your answer sheet.*

28　**The Aboriginal demand that bones be returned to Australia is based on which TWO ideas?**
　　A　The rightful place for the remains is Australia.
　　B　Britain had no right to take the remains.
　　C　The remains have religious significance for Aborigines.
　　D　Some remains have already been returned.
　　E　They believe the remains must be returned to their ancestors to find peace.

29　**Which TWO factors might cause problems when it comes to returning the remains?**
　　A　Scottish and English law does not allow museums to return objects.
　　B　It is not clear what will happen to the remains once they have been returned.
　　C　The remains are scientifically important and need to be studied.
　　D　Not all the Australian artifacts are human remains.
　　E　Some museums do not have the right to return objects to their countries of origin.

30　**Which TWO points may help to speed up the process of returning the remains?**
　　A　The British government is going to discuss the return of Aboriginal items.
　　B　Some items have already been returned to their countries of origin.
　　C　There is already some sympathy to the Aborigines' claims in the world of archeology.
　　D　Not all the Australian artifacts are human remains.
　　E　The remains have religious significance for Aborigines.

Questions 31 - 36

Classify the following opinions as referring to

　　A　The National College of Surgeons
　　B　Stevie McCoy
　　C　Dr William Cowell Bell
　　D　Lady Amanda Spurway
　　E　Ewan Mather
　　F　None of the above

*Write the appropriate letter **A - F** in boxes 31 - 36 on your answer sheet.*

31　No country would allow the bones of its citizens to be used for scientific purposes in another country.
32　The Glover Museum is ready to return its Aboriginal bones.
33　Australian remains are a useful resource for scientific study.
34　It would be a problem to accurately identify the human remains.
35　Most Aboriginal remains in Britain have been made into artifacts.
36　Discrepancies in the laws of different countries can hinder the return of relics.

Questions 37 - 40

*Complete the following paragraph based on information in Reading Passage 3 using **ONE** or **TWO WORDS** from the Reading Passage for each answer. Write your answers in boxes 37 - 40 on your answer sheet.*

Aborigines believe that the remains should be returned for a number of reasons. First is the fact that the relics were taken during the period when Australia was a .... (37). The Aborigine belief that their ancestors can only .... (38) if their bones are returned is a further factor. Thirdly, the restitution of the remains is an issue of human rights. However, objectors who oppose the return of the artifacts point out that not only is there a .... (39) problem, but also that the remains constitute an important .... (40) in studying the lifestyle of the Aborigines.

ACADEMIC WRITING
PRACTICE TEST 1

WRITING TASK 1

You should spend about 20 minutes on this task.

The graph below gives information about the progress of certain diseases during childhood between 1950 and 2000 in a developing country.

Write a report for a university lecturer describing the information shown below.

You should write at least 150 words.

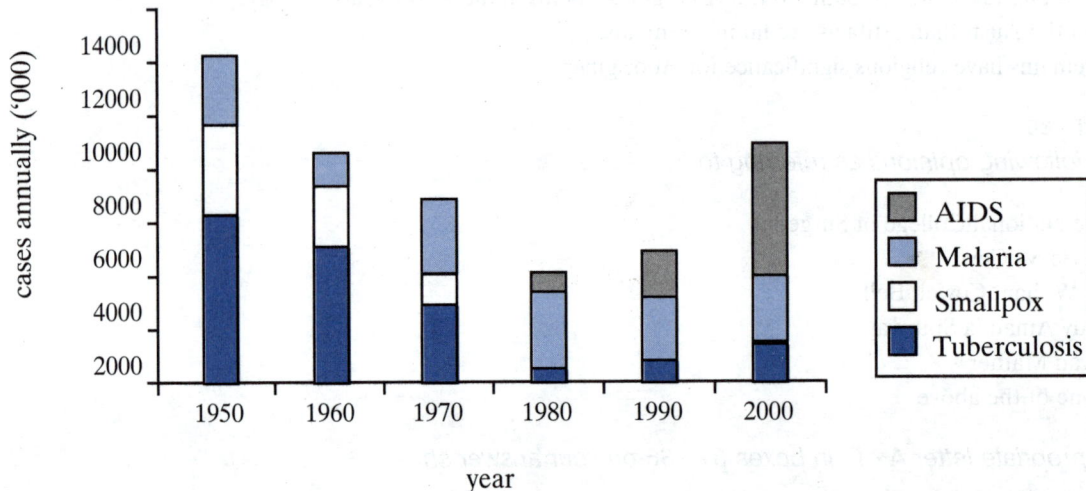

WRITING TASK 2

You should spend about 40 minutes on this task.

Present a written argument or case to an educated reader with no specialist knowledge of the following topic.

It has been claimed that workers over 50 are not responsive to rapidly changing ideas in the modern workplace and that for this reason younger workers are to be preferred.

To what extent would you support or reject this idea?

You should write at least 250 words.

You should use your own ideas, knowledge and experience and support your arguments with examples and relevant evidence.

SPEAKING
PRACTICE TEST 1

Part 1

I'd like you to tell me something about your family. Is that okay?

- Is your family large or small?
- What do the other members of the family do?
- When was the last time all your family were together? What did you do?
- What do you do as a family for special occasions like weddings or feasts?
- Is there a member of your family you are especially close to? Why?

Part 2

Describe a trip or a holiday you have recently taken.

Tell me about:
- where you went and why.
- who you went with.
- what you did, and
- what made this trip memorable to you.

- Had you been on a trip like this before?
- Why? Why not?
- Do you think travel broadens the mind?

Part 3

- travel
  - Describe how the tourism industry has developed in your area/other areas.
  - Describe what things your area offers tourists.
  - Evaluate what type of tourists tourism brings to your area.
  - How has tourism changed your area compared with how it used to be?
  - Evaluate how tourism is good for the economy of a country.
  - Speculate on what other benefits tourism might bring to a country.

- environmental and other problems
  - Evaluate how the growth of tourism has affected the countryside and wildlife in your area/country.
  - Discuss whether the advantages of tourism outweigh the disadvantages.

PRACTICE
TEST 2

LISTENING

PRACTICE TEST 2

NUMBER OF QUESTIONS: 40
APPROX. TIME: 30 MINUTES

Instructions

You will hear a number of conversations and talks and you must answer all the questions you hear. The conversations are recorded and you will have time to read the instructions and questions, and to check your work.

The tape will be played only ONCE.

The test is organised in 4 sections.

You can write your answers on the question paper and at the end of the test you will be given time to transfer your answers to an answer sheet.

Section 1 | Questions 1 - 10

Questions 1 - 2

Circle the correct answer **A - C**.

Example

The festival is about

A rivers.

B the inhabitants.

Ⓒ arts and music.

---

1 The festival lasts for

A 2 days.

B 3 days.

C 4 days.

2 It will take place on

A 14th July.

B 4th July.

C 4th August.

Questions 3 - 4

Circle **TWO** *answers* **A - E**.

You can buy tickets from

A the Town Hall.

B the festival office.

C libraries.

D tourist advice centres.

E post offices.

Questions 5 - 7

Write **NO MORE THAN THREE WORDS** *in each space.*

5 The weather forecast for the festival is ....

6 Food will be available from ....

7 There will be a bar selling soft drinks, ...

Questions 8 - 10

Write **ONE WORD** *in each space.*

Name of band	Where they come from	What kind of music
Petie's Dozen	.... (8)	Jazz
Strings	Poland	.... (9)
The Fiddlers	.... (10)	Folk

Section 2 | Questions 11 - 20

Questions 11 - 20
Write **A WORD** or **A NUMBER** in the spaces.

Current Account Overdraft Application Form

Surname: .... **(11)**

First name(s): .... **(12)**

Current Account no: 39261916

Address: 24, Kilverton Drive
.... **(13)**
SA3 9ER

Tel: 0458 88320

Date of birth: .... **(14)**

Work: Culver Engineering
30, ... **(15)**,
Carbury.

Tel: 0912 79509

Number of years in job: approx. 3 years

Current salary: .... **(16)**

Outgoings: Mortrgage: .... **(17)**
Credit cards: £45 .... **(18)**
                £19 storecards
Personal loans: .... **(19)**

Overdraft facility approved? Y / N
Overdraft limit: .... **(20)**

Section 3 Questions 21 - 30

Questions 21 - 23

Complete each sentence with **NO MORE THAN THREE WORDS** *or* **A NUMBER** *for each space.*

Student Union Elections

21 There are .... colleges in the university.
22 This election is held to choose .... student union officers.
23 Turnout last year was only .... per cent of those eligible to vote.

Questions 24 - 30

Complete the notes below. For questions 24 and 25 write **ONE WORD** *for each answer. For questions 26 - 30 write the letter* **A - D**. *Write* **A** *if Maria approves,* **B** *if David approves,* **C** *if both approve,* **D** *if neither approves.*

CANDIDATE	Good choice?
Jenny de Groot .... (24) Officer	.... (26)
Michael McCarthy Entertainments Officer	.... (27)
Wu Bing Lei Overseas Officer	.... (28)
Charles Law .... (25) Officer	.... (29)
Brian McKay Liaison Officer	.... (30)

Section 4 Questions 31 - 40

Questions 31 - 32
*Choose **TWO** answers.*

The main topics of the lecture are

A introduction to linguistics
B the history of European languages
C various languages
D how languages develop
E languages and evolution

Questions 33 - 40
*Write **NO MORE THAN THREE WORDS** for each space.*

33 Examples of natural languages are English, ...

34 In reality, natural languages are always ....

	PIDGIN	CREOLE
Origins	Came into being when two groups couldn't communicate in .... **(35)**	Developed from pidgin into .... **(36)**
Spoken	In Papua New Guinea, the Caribbean, ... **(38)**	In, for example, ... **(37)**
Features	Simplified form of one of the two groups' languages. Words have more .... **(39)**	As complex as natural languages. Have to fight to get the .... **(40)**

ACADEMIC READING
PRACTICE TEST 2

NUMBER OF QUESTIONS: 40
TIME PERMITTED: 1 HOUR

Instructions

WRITE ALL ANSWERS ON THE ANSWER SHEET

The test is organised as follows:

Reading Passage 1   Questions 1 - 15
Reading Passage 2   Questions 16 - 25
Reading Passage 3   Questions 26 - 40

Start at the beginning of the test and read the passages in order. Answer all the questions. If you are not sure of an answer, you can leave it and try to answer it later.

Section 1

You should spend about 20 minutes on questions 1 - 15, which are based on Reading Passage 1 below.

Sharks
—— *"Face Extinction"* ——

Professor Robert Law, head of Marine Biological Ltd, which monitors the ocean environment, and a leading governmental advisor on marine pollution, is claiming today that sharks are in danger of extinction. Professor Law's main point is that worldwide the number of sharks of most species is dropping rapidly. Exact figures about these elusive creatures are hard to come by, but the general consensus is that certain kinds of shark population have decreased by up to 75% in the last 30 years.

The great white and tiger sharks have seen the greatest drop in numbers, down by as much as 90% from 20 years ago. Smaller sharks are also under threat - the populations of makos, hammerheads, even common dogfish are being decimated. Estimates suggest that British dogfish numbers have halved in the last decade alone.

And this decline is worldwide. The big sharks congregate mainly in the warmer waters of the Pacific and Caribbean, but cold water areas such as the Atlantic and the North Sea have their own species and these too are in danger.

The reasons for the decline in numbers are not hard to see. One huge reason is the continued demand for shark fins in South-East Asia, where they are used to make soup and as ingredients in medicines. Most sharks that are killed commercially in the West are processed for the oil that comes from their livers. Sharks are also victims of fear, since they are routinely killed by fishermen when they are landed with other catches.

"Sharks have no protection," writes Professor Law. "They are not outside the law - most countries have laws protecting the species which are most under threat - but the problem is that people are so frightened of them that the laws are not enforced. There are perhaps five marine biologists in Europe actively involved in attempts to save shark species, although there is greater awareness in America and Australia. Sharks have an image problem. Nobody associates them with needing to be saved simply because they are such fearsome predators."

But the market demand for shark products has always been high. The real reason why shark stocks have plummeted is the same as the reason why other fish species are in decline. Modern fishing technology - the use of sonar and deep-netting in particular - has made the shark's natural defences useless.

Charles Starkling, author of *Jaws: the Myth of the Sea*, agrees. "The equipment the shark has to defend itself is perfect in the right environment. Against other sharks, humans, fish, all the normal dangers, the shark is virtually invincible." But Starkling adds that no animal, no matter how large and dangerous on its own, can fight against steel nets. "The nets that are put out to protect swimmers don't just keep sharks away. They kill them. A shark which is caught in a net dies, because sharks can't stop swimming. Without a swim bladder, the shark drowns as soon as it stops moving." Starkling says it is common practice for sharks to have their fins cut off by fishermen and then to be dropped back in the ocean alive. They die by drowning.

And the ecology of sharks makes them especially vulnerable. Sharks are top-of-the-chain predators, feeding on virtually anything else in the water, and consequently they are quite rare. For every million herring in the Atlantic, there will be one mako. Sharks are solitary and territorial, with unimaginably vast areas. The larger sharks also reproduce slowly, giving birth to live young one at a time.

Most people are afraid of sharks, but without good reason. You are many thousands of times more likely to be run over or die from smoking - even death by lightning or drowning in your bath are more likely - than to be attacked by a shark, and even then most shark attack victims survive. Recent research suggests that most sharks kill by mistake after taking an exploratory bite - humans are not sharks' chosen food. But time is running out for these ancient predators of the deeps. When their populations have gone below a certain level, no amount of legislation will protect them. Professor Law points out that most sharks cannot be kept in zoos, like tigers, and that once they are gone they will be gone forever. He counsels that sharks urgently need protection by law if they are to continue to grace the seas.

Questions 1 - 8

Complete the summary below. Choose your answers from the box below the summary and write them in boxes 1 - 8 on the answer sheet. There are more words than spaces, so you will not use all the given words.

Sharks Face Extinction

All over the world, shark populations are in dramatic .... **(1)**. In warm and cold waters, many shark species have been reduced to a .... **(2)** of their former size. This has come about largely as a result of the demand for shark products in the medical and catering industries, but sharks are also left biologically .... **(3)**, since they lack swim bladders and can drown if they are .... **(4)**. And the shark's reputation means it does not enjoy the .... **(5)** of other endangered species; conservation laws are often .... **(6)**. All these factors are compounded by recent .... **(7)** in the techniques of fishing. Sharks are comparatively rare, because of their status as .... **(8)**, and reproduce slowly. This makes them even more exposed to the dangers of overfishing. With stocks already very low, the time for full legal protection has come.

improvements	protection	decline	followed
fish	vulnerable	change	technology
ignored	section	attackers	laws
movement	trapped	open	part
predators	made	fraction	

Questions 9 - 15

*Do the following statements agree with the information given in Reading Passage 1? In boxes 9 - 15 on your answer sheet write **Yes** if the statement agrees with the information, **No** if the statement contradicts the information, **Not Given** if there is no information on this in the passage.*

9   We know precisely how much shark populations have declined.
10   The biggest reason for the decline of sharks is the demand for shark fins.
11   People are afraid to implement regulations safeguarding sharks.
12   The shark is able to protect itself in all circumstances.
13   Sharks live in groups.
14   Shark attacks are a statistically improbable cause of death for humans.
15   Sharks will become extinct in the near future.

Section 2

*You should spend about 20 minutes on questions **16 - 25**, which are based on Reading Passage 2 below.*

Water Power

Some of the ways in which Britain gets its energy are often dangerous and dirty. They are also unsustainable. Water power from the tides and the waves is one way to reduce pollution and create energy safely and cleanly.

More than 70% of the earth's surface is water. It is impossible to know exactly how much energy could be produced from this, although as an example 4-metre high waves in storms could produce up to 700 kilowatts per metre. While it is not practical to use stormy seas as a resource, even relatively calm seas and tidal rivers can be exploited for their energy potential.

Nowadays, machinery can be used to convert the power of moving water into electricity. In the past, a less efficient method was to use the power of the water directly in, for example, mills, where the falling water drove a wheel which simply drove the mill to convert corn to flour. Another alternative is to create a hydraulic ram, which sends water up a pipe to a higher level using only the power of the water itself.

Hydro-electricity is the most common use of water power in Britain, although even then it only accounts for 2% of all the electricity generated in Britain. A huge body of water, the reservoir, is held back by a dam so the water is fed through pipes at great speed, to a turbine which generates electricity. There are major advantages to this system. First, it is a clean source of power which uses only natural renewable resources. It is safe, too, if it is well-constructed, although there have been disasters when dams have burst. It is also possible to control how much power is generated. The major disadvantage, especially in Britain, which is comparatively small and overpopulated, is that hydro-electric power uses lots of land, which has to be flooded to make reservoirs. It also has very high start-up costs.

However, small-scale hydro-electric projects have fewer disadvantages than the huge schemes such as the Hoover Dam in the USA. They are cheaper to build and less potentially dangerous. This kind of smaller project uses turbines, which work on a similar principle to old-fashioned waterwheels, but are smaller and more efficient.

With impulse turbines, water is forced through pipes at speed. It hits specially-designed sections of a wheel, which spin. The kinetic energy thus produced is transferred to the engine. There are various kinds of impulse turbines, including the Pelton Turbine, which is a single or double width of cup-shaped devices on a narrow wheel, and the Cross-Flow Turbine, which consists of thin paddles on a long shaft, and which is suitable for wider areas.

There are also reaction turbines such as the Francis Turbine, which looks rather like a ship's propeller. They consist of a series of blades mounted inside the pipe which is carrying the water under great pressure. These blades are turned by the flow of water across them.

Small water turbines are only ever about 80% efficient, as some efficiency is inevitably lost in the transfer of energy. But this should not prevent us exploiting the power of water further. The small-scale systems described here are cheap and clean, and, once set-up costs have been met, will provide power for years to come without much maintenance and at no permanent cost to the environment.

Questions 16 - 21

*Label the diagrams below. Choose **NO MORE THAN THREE WORDS** from Reading Passage 2 for each answer. Write your answers in boxes 16 - 21 on your answer sheet.*

DIAGRAMS

.... (19)

.... (16)

.... (17)

.... (18)

.... (20)

.... (21)

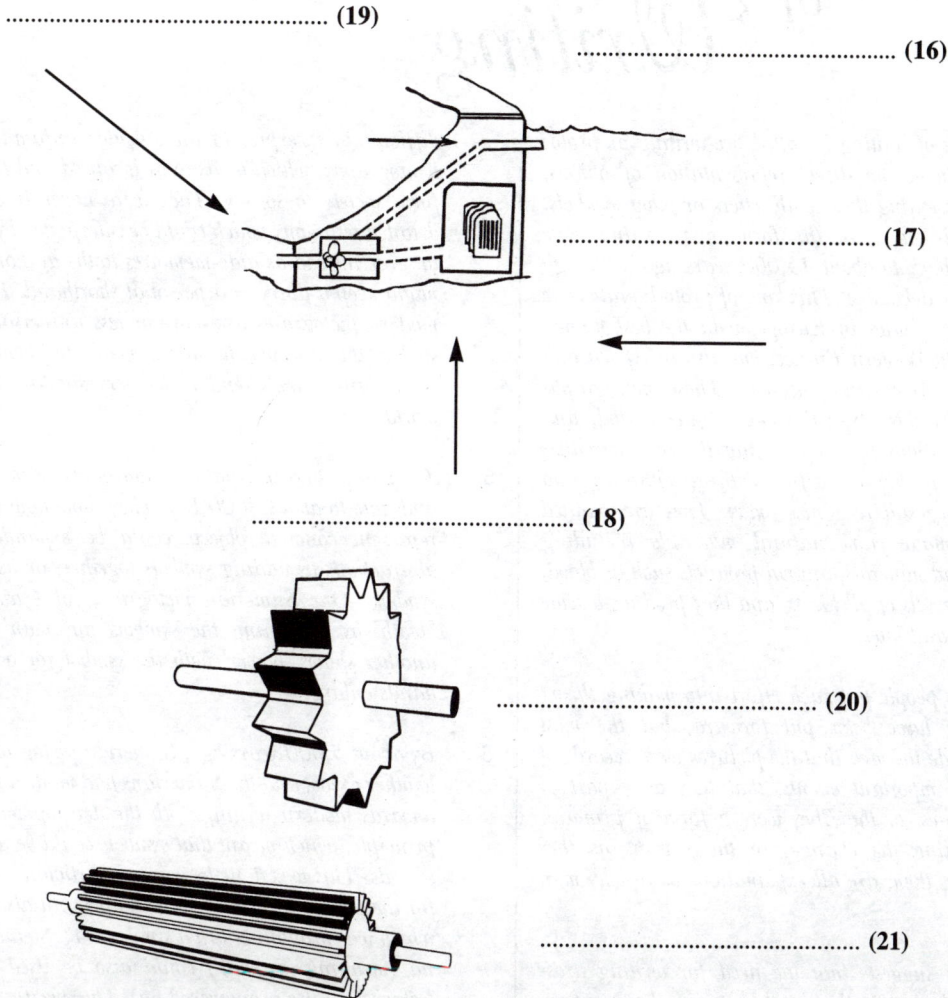

Questions 22 - 25

*Complete each of the following statements with words taken from Reading Passage 2. Write **NO MORE THAN THREE WORDS** for each answer. Write your answers in boxes 22 - 25 on your answer sheet.*

22 Using water power to move machinery is .... than using it to generate electricity.

23 About 20% of energy .... with smaller water turbines.

24 All water turbines rely on water being .... at great speed.

25 The main expense of hydro-electric projects lies in ....

Section 3

*You should spend about 20 minutes on questions **26 - 40**, which are based on Reading Passage 3 below.*

The History of Writing

1   The earliest stage of writing is called pre-writing or proto-literacy, and depends on direct representation of objects, rather than representing them with letters or other symbols. Evidence for this stage, in the form of rock and cave paintings, dates back to about 15,000 years ago, although the exact dates are debatable. This kind of proto-literate cave painting has been found in Europe, with the best known examples in South-Western France, but also in Africa and on parts of the American continent. These petrographs (pictures on rock) show typical scenes of the period, and include representations of people, animals and activities. Most are astonishingly beautiful, with a vibrancy and immediacy that we still recognise today. They are painted with pigments made from natural materials including crushed stones and minerals, animal products such as blood, ashes, plant materials of all kinds, and they produce a wide range of colours and hues.

2   Why did ancient people put such effort into making them? Various theories have been put forward, but the most compelling include the idea that the pictures were records of heroic deeds or important events, that they were part of magical ceremonies, or that they were a form of primitive calendar, recording the changes in the seasons as they happened. These, then, are all explanations as to why man started to write.

3   A related theory suggests that the need for writing arose thereafter from the transactions and bartering that went on. In parts of what is now Iraq and Iran, small pieces of fired earth - pottery - have been found which appear to have been used as tokens to represent bartered objects, much as we use tokens in a casino, or money, today. Eventually, when the tokens themselves became too numerous to handle easily, representations of the tokens were inscribed on clay tablets.

4   An early form of writing is the use of pictograms, which are pictures used to communicate. Pictograms have been found from almost every part of the world and every era of development, and are still in use in primitive communities nowadays. They represent objects, ideas or concepts more or less directly. They tend to be simple in the sense that they are not a complex or full picture, although they are impressively difficult to interpret to an outsider unfamiliar with their iconography, which tends to be localised and to differ widely form society to society. They were never intended to be a detailed testimony which could be interpreted by outsiders, but to serve instead as aide-memoires to the author, rather as we might keep a diary in a personal shorthand. However, some modern pictograms are more or less universally recognised, such as the signs which indicate men's and women's toilets, or road signs, which tend to be very similar throughout the world.

5   The first pictograms that we know of are Sumerian in origin, and date to about 8000 BC. They show how images used to represent concrete objects could be expanded to include abstractions by adding symbols together, or using associated symbols. One Sumerian pictogram, for example, indicates 'death' by combining the symbols for 'man' and 'winter'; another shows 'power' with the symbol for a man with the hands enlarged.

6   By about 5,000 years ago, Sumerian pictograms had spread to other areas, and the Sumerians had made a major advance towards modern writing with the development of the rebus principle, which meant that symbols could be used to indicate sounds. This was done by using a particular symbol not only for the thing it originally represented, but also for any thing which was pronounced in a similar way. So the pictogram for na (meaning 'animal') could also be used to mean 'old' (which was also pronounced na). The specific meaning of the pictogram (whether na meant 'old' or 'animal') could only be decided through its context.

7   It is a short step from this to the development of syllabic writing using pictograms, and this next development took about another half a century. Now the Sumerians would add pictograms to each other, so that each, representing an individual sound - or syllable - formed part of a larger word. Thus pictograms representing the syllables he, na and mi ('mother', 'old', 'my') could be put together to form henami or 'grandmother'.

Questions 26 - 32

Reading Passage 3 has seven paragraphs 1 - 7. Choose the most suitable headings for paragraphs 1 - 7 from the list of headings below. Write the appropriate letters A - H in boxes 26 - 32 on your answer sheet. There are more headings than paragraphs, so you will not use them all.

Paragraph Headings

A Magic and Heroes	**D** Sounds and Symbols	**G** A Personal Record
B Doing Business	**E** Images on Stone	**H** From Visual to Sound
C Early Developments	**F** Stories and Seasons	

26   Paragraph 1   29   Paragraph 4   32   Paragraph 7   ....

27   Paragraph 2   30   Paragraph 5   ....

28   Paragraph 3   31   Paragraph 6   ....

Questions 33 - 37

Complete the following notes on Reading Passage 3 using ONE or TWO WORDS from the Reading Passage for each answer. Write your answers in boxes 33 - 37 on your answer sheet.

Notes on the Development of Writing

First stage of writing - pre-writing or proto-literacy – very old – 15,000 years. Evidence: cave and rock paintings. Famous example - .... **(33)**. Reasons for development of writing: primitive ceremonies, recording events, seasons, used on pottery to represent .... **(34)** . Next stage: simple pictograms – pictures used to represent articles and .... **(35)**. Very simple drawings (but very difficult to understand). Then – 8000 BC – combined .... **(36)** to create new concepts (eg. man + winter = death). After this - started using same pictogram for different words with same .... **(37)**. Very important step.

Questions 38 - 40

Choose the appropriate letters A - D and write them in boxes 38 - 40 on your answer sheet.

38   The earliest stages of writing
   A wcrc discovered 15,000 years ago and are found all over the world.
   B are pictures which show the natural life of the time.
   C are called petrographs and were painted with natural materials.
   D could not describe concepts.

39   The earliest pictograms
   A represent complex objects and are difficult to understand.
   B represent comparatively simple objects and are easy to understand.
   C are a record of events for outsiders.
   D are fairly simple but may not be easy to interpret.

40   About 5,000 years ago
   A Sumerians were developing sounds.
   B Sumerians were writing in a modern style.
   C pictograms were used over a wide area.
   D pictogram symbols could only have one meaning.

ACADEMIC WRITING
PRACTICE TEST 2

WRITING TASK 1

You should spend about 20 minutes on this task.

The following table shows preferences for academic subjects studied at degree level in different countries.

Write a report for a university lecturer describing the information shown below.

You should write at least 150 words.

Subjects studied at university

Australia		UK		France	
Medicine	10%	Media Studies	15%	Engineering	18%
History	8%	Literature	12%	Medicine	6%
Sports science	8%	Sports science	12%	Law	6%
Law	5%	Law	10%	Languages	6%
Engineering	3%	Medicine	4%	Literature	4%
Languages	2%	Languages	1%	History	2%
Literature	1%	Engineering	1%	Sports science	0%

WRITING TASK 2

You should spend about 40 minutes on this task.

Present a written argument or case to an educated reader with no specialist knowledge of the following topic.

The international community should reduce or eliminate the debts of the world's poorest countries.

To what extent would you support or reject this proposal?

You should write at least 250 words.

You should use your own ideas, knowledge and experience and support your arguments with examples and relevant evidence.

SPEAKING
PRACTICE TEST 2

Part 1

I'd like you to tell me something about your studies and career. Is that okay?

– Are you studying, or do you have a job?

Work
– What job do you do?
– Have you always been/done that?
– What made you choose that job?
– What are the things you like about it?
– What things don't you like about it?

Study
– What exactly are you studying?
– Have you been studying it for a long time?
– Why did you choose to study it?
– Are you enjoying the course? Why?/Why not?

Part 2

Describe a film you've seen recently.

Tell me about:
– what happened in the film,
– the atmosphere of the film,
– whether you enjoyed it,
and you should say why you chose to talk about this film.

– Does your country have a flourishing film industry?
– What kind of films are popular in your country?

Part 3

- Films
  - What do you think makes a good film?
  - Evaluate the influence of violence in films on young people.
  - Compare the films made in your country with Hollywood films.

- Music
  - Compare modern music and traditional music in your country.
  - Speculate how music can bring people together.
  - Describe the most popular musicians/form of music in your country.

PRACTICE
TEST 3

LISTENING
PRACTICE TEST 3

NUMBER OF QUESTIONS: 40
APPROX. TIME: 30 MINUTES

Instructions

You will hear a number of conversations and talks and you must answer all the questions you hear. The conversations are recorded and you will have time to read the instructions and questions, and to check your work.

The tape will be played only ONCE.

The test is organised in 4 sections.

You can write your answers on the question paper and at the end of the test you will be given time to transfer your answers to an answer sheet.

Section 1 Questions 1 - 10

Questions 1 - 10

Complete the following notes using **A WORD** *or* **SHORT PHRASE** *for each answer.*

<table>
<tr><td colspan="4" align="center">**Borchester University**</td></tr>
<tr><td colspan="4">**Example:**   **Where to get** ...*food*... **on campus**</td></tr>
<tr><td>**PLACE**</td><td>**CAPACITY**</td><td>**REGULAR MENU**</td><td>**COST**</td></tr>
<tr>
<td>Main Refectory Hall
Open .... **(2)**</td>
<td>500</td>
<td>vegetarian, fish
.... **(1)**</td>
<td>..................................... **(3)** – £3</td>
</tr>
<tr>
<td>Arts Building Café
Open: 9 - 6</td>
<td>.................. **(4)**</td>
<td>tea, coffee, hot
chocolate, sandwiches</td>
<td>..................................... **(5)**</td>
</tr>
<tr>
<td>..................................... **(6)** Bar
Open: 10 - 4</td>
<td></td>
<td>tea, coffee,
.... **(7)**
sandwiches</td>
<td>£1.30</td>
</tr>
</table>

Questions 8 - 10

Complete the sentences below. Write **NO MORE THAN THREE WORDS** *for each answer.*

8 You can hear a concert of classical music every ....

9 The jazz concerts start at ....

10 You can smoke in ....

Section 2 Questions 11 - 20

Questions 11 - 17
Complete Amanda's notes in **NO MORE THAN THREE WORDS** *for each answer.*

WHERE TO SEND OUR RUBBISH

ITEM	WHERE?
Returnable glass bottles	milkman, ... (11)
.... (12)	glass container
Telephone books	.... (13)
Paperbacks	.... (14)
.... (15)	general rubbish — no recycling
Newspapers	.... (16) container
.... (17)	charity shop

Questions 18 - 20
Write **NO MORE THAN THREE WORDS** *for each answer.*

18   How will Amanda and Barry know where to put the different plastic bottles?
....

19   What does the technician do?
....

20   Who uses the clothes which are in bad condition?
....

Section 3 | Questions 21 - 30

Questions 21 - 24

Circle the correct answer **A - D**.

21 Roughly what proportion of the public is happy with the hospital?
   A all
   B the vast majority
   C few
   D some

22 What is the purpose of the "Visitors' Charter"?
   A To notify the public.
   B To display standards.
   C To help patients with special needs.
   D To give patients a sympathetic ear.

23 What is the purpose of the "sympathetic ear" symbol on patient records?
   A To make the patient aware of the problem.
   B To impair hearing.
   C To gain the patients' consent.
   D To indicate a patient who has difficulty hearing.

24 The work on the main entrance
   A will be improved.
   B will be completed on schedule.
   C will be finished in a few months.
   D will cost more than planned.

Questions 25 - 27

Complete the sentences below. Write **NO MORE THAN THREE WORDS** *for each answer.*

25 Members of staff who know a foreign language ought to have .... to
    indicate this.
26 The hospital has bilingual staff speaking Welsh, Urdu and ....
27 The hospital hopes more languages will be offered in ....

Questions 28 and 29

Circle **TWO** *answers* **A - E**.

   Which ideas will the hospital use for fundraising?
   A camping
   B outdoor suppers
   C sponsored bikes in the park
   D sponsored swims
   E surveys

Question 30

Circle the correct answer **A - D**.

30 How many people completed the questionnaire?
   A   18   B   150   C   200   D   98

Section 4 | Questions 31 - 40

Questions 31 - 38

Complete the questionnaire below. Write **NO MORE THAN THREE WORDS** *or* **A NUMBER** *for each answer.*

Borchester University
Module Assessment Feedback Questionnaire

Underline level: <u>Level 1</u>   Level 2   Level 3

Title of Module: *An Introduction to* .... **(31)**

Name of tutors: *Professor Merrick and* .... **(32)**

Underline type of teaching: lecture   practical   seminar   **(33)**
                                 other (please specify)

Please score on the following scale: 1 = strongly disagree
                                         2 = disagree
                                         3 = agree
                                         4 = strongly agree

1   The module has clearly stated aims and objectives.   [4]

2   Teaching methods are well chosen.   .... **(34)**

3   The tutor presents module content clearly.   .... **(35)**

4   The teaching is well matched by an up-to-date reading list.   .... **(36)**

5   Book provision in the library is adequate.   .... **(37)**

6   Time on each topic/area is well distributed.   [4]

7   Assignment feedback is helpful.   .... **(38)**

8   Seminar/group work improves understanding.   [4]

9   Module stretches student's capacity for knowledge/skills/ideas.   [4]

Questions 39 and 40

Circle **TWO** *answers* **A - E**.

Which problems in the classroom did Ann and Geoff note down?

A   inadequate facilities

B   room too small

C   room too hot

D   room has too many people

E   chairs without wings

ACADEMIC READING
PRACTICE TEST 3

NUMBER OF QUESTIONS: 40

TIME PERMITTED: 1 HOUR

Instructions

WRITE ALL ANSWERS ON THE ANSWER SHEET

The test is organised as follows:

Reading Passage 1	*Questions 1 - 14*
Reading Passage 2	*Questions 15 - 26*
Reading Passage 3	*Questions 27 - 40*

Start at the beginning of the test and read the passages in order. Answer all the questions. If you are not sure of an answer, you can leave it and try to answer it later.

Section 1

*You should spend about 20 minutes on questions **1 - 14**, which are based on Reading Passage 1 below.*

Britain set for heat wave – in 2050!

A As you sit in your home or office and look at the rain running relentlessly down the window pane, you will almost certainly be thinking, "This is more like February, when will summer arrive?" This summer seems to have been colder and wetter than ever. So here is some good news. The Meteorological Office computer has analysed weather patterns over the last 100 years and suggests that the weather will get both drier and warmer - but in fifty year's time.

B Regardless of the effects of global warming it seems as though we can expect the average temperature in the UK to increase by 1.5°C. In parts of the UK we can also expect rainfall to decrease. Probably this will be most apparent in the south and east of Britain where rainfall is already the lowest in the UK. It looks as though parts of the UK may be prone to drought by the middle of the next century. This has already been noticed in the English wine making industry. John Gore Bullingham, who makes the award winning Carter Castle sparkling wine, has noticed that his grapes ripen two or three weeks earlier than they did when he started the vineyard in 1955.

C All of this seems hard to believe. At present we are in the middle of a cold, grey and distinctly sodden July. It seems as though summer will never arrive. How does this observation fit with Met Office predictions of a warmer, drier Britain? The Met Office's chief weather forecaster Claire Miles explains, "At present the weather over the whole of North America, the North Atlantic and Europe has become temporarily blocked. Those areas which have good weather, such as Southern Europe and the Balkans, can expect to keep it and develop heat waves. Those areas which have bad weather, such as the UK and Northern France, will keep the rain and unseasonable cold."

D We seem to have kept it for some time already. In the last two weeks of June and first two weeks of July the UK has had an average daily temperature of 12.9°C. Although it is hard to believe, this is only 1.7°C lower than normal for the time of year. But what makes it seem so cold is that in the same period there has been only three hours of sunshine a day; less than half the average for the period. This, combined with northerly winds, makes it seem much colder. It may get a little warmer towards the end of the month but not much.

E Blocked weather does not have to be bad for the UK. The glorious summer of 1976 was caused by the same phenomenon. In that case the weather patterns came to a standstill with hot rather than cold weather over the UK. Even now, parts of Europe are suffering their highest temperatures for a generation. In Athens last week the temperature rose to 48.5°C, a temperature record for Europe. The settled and warm weather which would normally come to Britain on prevailing westerly winds is now stuck over the North Atlantic, sandwiched between unusually cold and wet weather in Northern Europe and the East coast of North America.

F "Basically," says Miss Miles, "you've got low pressure centred on the UK and the eastern US and two huge high pressure areas centred on the Atlantic and the Balkans. Normally high altitude winds would blow west to east and bring the weather with them. They form waves so in somewhere like the UK we usually get alternate high and low pressure systems passing over us. These bring, successively, warm and sunny, then colder and wetter weather and there is a pretty fixed boundary between the two. But this year the waves have been more pronounced. The waves become so big they turn into cells with the winds within them going round in circles. The normal west to east winds stop and the weather remains static for some time. It could stay like this for the whole summer."

Questions 1 - 5

Reading Passage 1 has six paragraphs **A - F**. *Choose the most suitable headings for paragraphs A - F from the list of headings below. Write the appropriate number i - viii in boxes 1 - 5 on your answer sheet. The first one has been done for you as an example.*

There are more headings than paragraphs, so you will not use them all.

Paragraph Headings

i)	The Process of Blocked Patterns	**v)**	The Weather Now and in the Future
ii)	Better Weather in Britain Soon	**vi)**	The Weather Now
iii)	The Highs and Lows of Weather	**vii)**	Met Office Forecasts
iv)	Record UK Temperatures	**viii)**	Weather Blocking in the Past

Example   Paragraph A   ....

1	Paragraph B	....	**3**	Paragraph D	....
2	Paragraph C	....	**4**	Paragraph E	....

5 Paragraph F   ....

Questions 6 - 12

Complete the notes below which summarise the explanation for blocked weather patterns using answers selected from the box below. Write your answers on the answer sheet.

alternately	usually	occasionally	always	never	speed up
bigger	rotate	still	block	smaller	

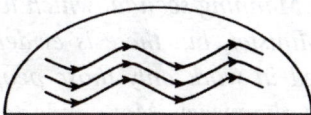

.... **(6)**, very high winds blow west to east. These form waves which bring .... **(7)** good and bad weather systems with them.

.... **(8)**, these waves become .... **(9)** and at the highest point and lowest points of the waves the air begins to .... **(10)**.

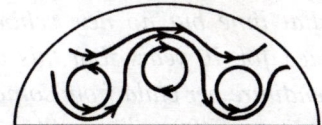

The circling air forms cells which .... **(11)** the usual streams of air across the Atlantic ocean. With no high winds these cells stay .... **(12)** for some time.

Questions 13 - 14

Complete the following paragraph based on information in Reading Passage 1 using **NO MORE THAN THREE WORDS** *from the Reading Passage for each answer. Write the answers in boxes 13 - 14 on your answer sheet.*

The weather in Britain is expected to change in the next fifty years. The temperatures will rise and in some areas the amount of rain will certainly .... **(13)**. Indeed it has been forecast that some regions of England will be .... **(14)** by 2050.

*You should spend about 20 minutes on questions **15 - 26**, which are based on Reading Passage 2 below.*

The **Biggest** Australian **Budget** Ever

The Australian government is set to announce some of the biggest ever spending increases in education, welfare, the foreign office and defence at lunchtime tomorrow. After a decade of strong industrial growth, record low unemployment and a booming economy, the government feels confident enough to reinvest some of the funds it has been hoarding since it came to power four years ago.

In accordance with the priorities which were stated when the Liberal party was elected, a very sizeable portion of this bounty will go to education and to schools in particular. Approximately A$1 billion is expected to go on educational building through the Neighbourhood Renewal Scheme. School buildings have suffered shameful neglect for over half a century. The population has grown and education has changed in that time but no new school buildings have been erected for 10 years. But this change should increase expenditure per child from some A$350 to over A$700. A further A$400 million will go on increasing teachers' pay. There is national shortage of teachers, especially in areas such as science, mathematics and religion. The target to increase teachers in training to 5,600 last year was missed by a huge margin; only 2,533 actually enrolled. Increases both in basic pay and in incentive schemes, such as rewards for conspicuous achievement and cash payments for trainee teachers, will be made.

In contrast to last year, expenditure on health will rise by less than one per cent and the changes here will be in research funding. The most notable change is in funding to the Adelaide Epidemiology Centre which is nearing its goal of marketing a vaccination against AIDS. The Department of Health will inject A$5.8 million for the large-scale, double-blind trials it requires. This compares with A$575,000 invested by the government in this programme last year. A government spokesman explains that, "health will be taking a back seat this year because of the huge increases announced in this area over the previous two years."

In other areas significant changes are also occurring. In the Department of Pensions and Welfare, state old age pensions, frozen at A$204 per month for the last three years are set to rise to A$255 per month. Unemployment benefit, likewise frozen for three years, is also set to rise but not until next year. Thereafter, rises of 10.5% over each of the remaining three years of this Parliament are scheduled. This is not as generous as it may seem, however, as certain categories of expenditure will be phased out. The Work Now Scheme to encourage single mothers back into the labour market will go, as will the infamous YTCs. The Youth Training Councils received a bad press over the Manning scandal which led to the resignation of the Minister, but there is evidence that these schemes placed in work only those people who would have found work anyway. More importantly, the period over which unemployment benefit is paid has been cut from a year to eight months and this might remove 20% of all claimants.

In Defence and the Foreign Office, there are increases in the funding of the Voice of Australia radio service. The A$128 million may seem a small investment but it checks the reduction in funds from A$2 billion to A$698 million over the last decade which threatened to end the service entirely. A$500 million is being made available for two new warships and a further A$250 million for an extension to the Rapid Reaction Force now seen as so much more important given recent political and civil unrest in Indonesia, Malaysia, Papua New Guinea and Fiji.

Questions 15 - 21

For questions 15 - 21 match the statistical changes stated in the text with a numerical expression . Write your answers in boxes 15 - 21 on your answer sheet. There are more expressions than answers needed, so you will not use them all.

double	twelvefold	one in five	one in ten
less than half	about a third	about one in six	6%
tenfold	25%	10.5%	12%

15 The decrease in financial support for the Voice of Australia over the previous 10 years ....

16 The shortfall in the numbers who entered teacher training ....

17 The long term increase in unemployment benefit ....

18 The reduction in the numbers eligible for unemployment benefit ....

19 The increase in funding for AIDS research ....

20 The increase in state pensions ....

21 The increase in per capita expenditure on schools ....

Questions 22 - 26

Do the following statements agree with the information given in Reading Passage 2? In boxes 22 - 26 on your answer sheet write **Yes** *if the statement agrees with the information,* **No** *if the statement contradicts the information,* **Not Given** *if there is no information on this in the passage.*

22 The Australian government has been increasing expenditure for four years.

23 School buildings have been neglected for 10 years.

24 The Work Now Scheme was unsuccessful.

25 The state pension did not increase for three years.

26 The government has decided to release some of its reserves to improve the lives of its citizens.

You should spend about 20 minutes on questions 27 - 40, which are based on Reading Passage 3 below.

A MAN OF PRINCIPLE
OR NEEDLESS MARTYR?

Sir Thomas More was the most brilliant Englishman of his age in an age, the early Renaissance, which is thought to be particularly brilliant. He scaled the heights in law, in philosophy and literature, and attained high political rank as Chancellor. But the most challenging thing about this man is nothing that he achieved in life but the nature of his death. The facts are well known. He was executed by King Henry VIII in 1534 for refusing to accept Henry as head of the church in England. What is unclear is why he chose to refuse, and to die, in this way.

Clouding the issue are the political and religious arguments which were at the root of his refusal and his death. It will be remembered that King Henry VIII was, for most of his life, an ardent Catholic who was awarded the title of *Defender of the Faith* for his resistance to the Protestant reformation. But his desperation for a male heir led Henry to divorce his first wife, Catherine of Aragon, in favour of the younger Ann Boleyn who offered the promise of a son. High politics among the crowned heads of Europe meant that this could only be achieved by a break with Rome and the acceptance of Protestantism in England. In a time when religion was taken very seriously by whole populations there was bound to be resistance.

Traditional Catholic writers, such as Friar Anthony Foley, have cast More as a martyr who stood up for the cause of Catholicism and perished for the true religion. "More was a beacon of light in those dark times," says Friar Foley, "whose actions have shown the path of righteousness for true believers even down to the present day." This interpretation was convenient for the Catholic church, then as now, and resulted in More being made a saint. It ignores, however, the fact that More took every step to stop his ideas being made a political issue. Whatever reason he had it was not support of the Catholic church. It also does not explain why More chose to take a stand, and effectively commit suicide, on this issue. Even under the teachings of the Catholic church he could have sworn the necessary oath to Henry because he was under duress. The church in his day did not expect or require him to refuse. More's personal beliefs were his own but refusal to take the oath is what condemned him.

A more recent biography, by Paul Hardy, views More as a medieval man and not the renaissance man he is often seen as. As such, Hardy argues, he would have been deeply conservative. The changes which Henry was embracing, with the acceptance of Protestantism, would have been highly offensive. "As a lawyer and Chancellor, More had spent his life defending the status quo and now, at the stroke of a pen, it was turned round," he writes. This rather ignores the deliberate modernity which imbued every other aspect of More's life from legal reform to the rewriting of school textbooks.

Other writers, such as the psychotherapist Bill Blake, see More's demise as an example of depressive illness. Melancholy was widely known at the time but not seen as an illness. It is not implausible that under the strain of work and the profile of his position as Chancellor, he succumbed to depression and, desperate and indecisive, let death sweep over him. But contemporary reports are at odds with this. He made every effort to comfort and cheer up his own relatives and never appeared lost or undecided.

Since More himself left no explanation we will probably never really know what his motivation was. However, Hardy's observations are very true in some respects in that More lived in a very different world and one that is hard for us to understand. Life could be very cheap 500 years ago especially if one held high political office or intellectual views at odds with the establishment. There is no better way of appreciating this than to consider the fate of the poets in the *Oxford Book of Sixteenth Century Verse*. Two thirds of these poets died violent deaths, almost all at the hands of an executioner. With the possibility of death ever present it seems to have been regarded then with something less than the dread it evokes today. Perhaps this is what happened with More. After a lifetime of good fortune, considerable luxury and achievement, the wheel of fortune had turned, and he accepted his fate with good grace in the hope of an even better life in the hereafter.

Questions 27 - 34

Classify the following statements as referring to

Writers

A   Foley   D   The writer of the article
B   Hardy   E   Contemporary writers
C   Blake

Example	Answer
More took a religious stand against Protestantism.	A

Write the appropriate letters in boxes 27 - 33 on your answer sheet. You may use any answer more than once.

27   More was suffering from depression when he died.
28   More was a traditionalist in his views.
29   More could have taken the oath and remained a Catholic.
30   More had a positive attitude to life and helped others.
31   More was defending the true faith.
32   More resigned himself to the fact that his good luck had changed.
33   More had a lifestyle which is difficult for modern man to comprehend.
34   More showed he was a modern man in his restructuring of the law and education.

Questions 35 - 40

*For questions 35 - 40, choose the best answers, **A, B, C** or **D**, according to the information in the text. Write your answers on the answer sheet.*

35   Henry VIII executed More because
  A   Henry VIII wanted a son.
  B   More believed in Protestantism.
  C   More was Chancellor.
  D   More refused to take an oath.

36   More's death is a mystery because
  A   he chose to be executed.
  B   he left no written explanation.
  C   the facts of his death are not known.
  D   it is bound up in religious controversy.

37   Which of the following was More NOT expert in?
  A   literature
  B   religion
  C   philosophy
  D   law

38   The writer disbelieves traditional views of More's death because
  A   More committed suicide.
  B   More didn't follow Catholic teaching in refusing the oath.
  C   theories of depression are more persuasive.
  D   little is really understood of the time More lived in.

39   According to the writer, the life of an intellectual 500 years ago could be dangerous
  A   because the standard of living was cheap.
  B   because they held high political office.
  C   if they held dissident views.
  D   if they suffered from depression.

40   Henry VIII broke from Rome because
  A   he believed Protestantism was the true faith.
  B   Rome refused him a divorce.
  C   he wanted to ensure the succession.
  D   he wanted to marry Ann Boleyn.

ACADEMIC WRITING
PRACTICE TEST 3

WRITING TASK 1

You should spend about 20 minutes on this task.

The table below shows the total appearances in court or 10 to 18 year old children distinguished by age and sex in New South Wales, Australia between July 1994 and June 1995.

Write a report for a university lecturer describing the information shown below.

You should write at least 150 words.

Age	10	11	12	13	14	15	16	17	18
Boys	25	90	238	602	1286	2060	2915	3495	1203
Girls	4	3	38	135	300	530	586	596	163

WRITING TASK 2

You should spend about 40 minutes on this task.

Present a written argument or case to an educated reader with no specialist knowledge of the following topic.

Tourism is a modern form of colonialism. It distorts local economies, causes environmental damage and ruins the places it exploits.

To what extent would you support or reject this idea?

You should write at least 250 words.

You should use your own ideas, knowledge and experience and support your arguments with examples and relevant evidence.

SPEAKING
PRACTICE TEST 3

Part 1

I'd like you to tell me something about your English studies. Is that okay?

- Why are you learning English?
- When did you start learning English?
- Which aspects of English do you find the most difficult?
- What parts of learning English do you enjoy?
- How important is English in your country?

Part 2

Describe a place you have visited in your country which is famous for its beauty.

Tell me about:
- where it is in your country,
- what it looks like,
- why it is important in your country,
and explain why you have chosen this place.

- Do you like to travel in your country?
- Do you think it is important to take regular holidays?

Part 3

- cities and towns
  - Describe the biggest city in your country.
  - Compare life in this city with life in the countryside.
  - Describe how city life will change in the future.

- transport
  - Describe the public transport system in your country.
  - Compare public and private transport.
  - Describe the pros and cons of air travel.

- pollution
  - Discuss the effects of industrialisation in your country.
  - Evaluate the levels of pollution in your country.

PRACTICE
TEST 4

LISTENING

PRACTICE TEST 4

NUMBER OF QUESTIONS: 40
APPROX. TIME: 30 MINUTES

Instructions

You will hear a number of conversations and talks and you must answer all the questions you hear. The conversations are recorded and you will have time to read the instructions and questions, and to check your work.

The tape will be played only ONCE.

The test is organised in 4 sections.

You can write your answers on the question paper and at the end of the test you will be given time to transfer your answers to an answer sheet.

Section 1 | Questions 1 - 10

Questions 1 - 8

Complete the notes below. Write NO MORE THAN THREE WORDS for each answer.

TOUR OF EUROPEAN CAPITALS

Leader: Jenny Allen

Driver: Ray .... (1)

Duration: .... (2) days

DAY ONE

Wolverhampton → London	arrive	1:00		lunch
		3:00		.... (3)
		5:00		book into hotel
		.... (4)		theatre trip
		11:00		back at hotel
		[can have something to .... (5)]		

DAY TWO

London → .... (6)	7:00	breakfast
	9:30	Eurostar
	1:00	book into Hotel .... (7)
	5:00 – .... (8)	free time
	8:30	dinner

Questions 9 and 10

Write NO MORE THAN THREE WORDS for each answer.

9 Why is there no tour of Brussels?

....

10 What will the group be visiting in Amsterdam?

....

Section 2 | Questions 11 - 20

Questions 11 - 14
Complete the notes below. Write **NO MORE THAN THREE WORDS** *for each answer.*

BUSINESS PLANNING EXERCISE

FORM: PRESENTATION WITH .... **(11)**

STUDENT	TASK	WHY?
Mark	financial .... **(12)**	good at figures
Andrew	helping Mark	.... **(13)** with figures
Jessica	helping Debbie	good research skills
Debbie	research .... **(14)**	good research skills

Questions 15 - 18
Complete the sentences below. Write **NO MORE THAN THREE WORDS** *for each answer.*

15   The presentation will be in .... weeks.
16   Jessica cannot work on the presentation next week because she'll be ....
17   Most of the basic work on the project will be done by ....
18   The meeting to discuss the progress of the project will take place on ....

Questions 19 and 20
Choose the best answer **A - D**.

19   **What time will the final meeting take place?**
     A   11:00
     B   12:00
     C   1:00
     D   2:00

20   **Who will present the final talk?**
     A   a Japanese student
     B   Mark
     C   Jessica
     D   no one chosen yet

Section 3 | Questions 21 - 27

Questions 21 - 27

Complete the interviewer's notes below. Write **NO MORE THAN THREE WORDS** *for each answer.*

INTERVIEW NOTES

Position: Assistant in languages department
Interviewer: Mrs Davis

Applicant: .... **(21)** Barracco

Appointment: [changed day – has to meet .... **(22)**]
now .... **(23)**

Application form already received and checked: Yes ☐ No ☐ **(24)**

English Level: Fair (Good) Excellent

Work Experience: Worked in a bank .... **(25)**

To teach: ENGLISH / (ITALIAN) / RUSSIAN

Commitments: Applied for place on .... **(26)**

Details of teaching position: Teach course on .... **(27)**

Questions 28 - 30

Write **NO MORE THAN THREE WORDS** *for each answer.*

28 What is the interviewee particularly concerned about?

....

29 Where will the interviewee live?

....

30 When will the interviewee find out if she will be employed as a teaching assistant?

....

Section 4 Questions 31 - 40

Questions 31 - 32
*Circle the correct answer **A - D.***

31 Tonight's ceremony is mainly
    A to celebrate the centenary of the college.
    B to celebrate the achievements of the college over 100 years.
    C to present a prize to the college.
    D to present prizes to the students.

32 Government figures show that the college's main strengths are
    A teaching, research and care for students.
    B research and engineering.
    C teaching and engineering.
    D engineering research and care for students.

Questions 33 - 36
*Complete each sentence in **NO MORE THAN THREE WORDS.***

33 In 1900, the area's traditional industries were .... and agriculture.
34 The college originally wanted to help .... from the town and local area.
35 Dr Bart Halliday is .... for winning the Nobel Prize.
36 By 1917 it was producing .... a year.

Questions 37 - 40
*Write a shrot answer to these questions using **NO MORE THAN THREE WORDS**.*

37 Why didn't Lucian Dewdley finish his studies? ....
38 What invention brought fame to the college? ....
39 In which other areas has the college become renowned? ....
40 How long has the speaker been Principal of the College? ....

ACADEMIC READING

PRACTICE TEST 4

NUMBER OF QUESTIONS: 40
TIME PERMITTED: 1 HOUR

Instructions

WRITE ALL ANSWERS ON THE ANSWER SHEET

The test is organised as follows:

Reading Passage 1	*Questions 1 - 13*
Reading Passage 2	*Questions 14 - 27*
Reading Passage 3	*Questions 28 - 40*

Start at the beginning of the test and read the passages in order. Answer all the questions. If you are not sure of an answer, you can leave it and try to answer it later.

Section 1

You should spend about 20 minutes on questions 1 - 13, which are based on Reading Passage 1 below.

The **Brain** and **Intelligence**

Human intelligence is an elusive quality. We all think we know it when we see it but try to pin down that quality to a firm, testable definition and suddenly, even for the most experienced researchers, the concept disappears. But now a team of British and German scientists believe they have firmly nailed down at least part of the notion of intelligence. They claim to have found a location for intelligence, whatever it is, in the brain.

For many years researchers have believed that intelligence is a quality which is spread throughout the whole human brain. Traditional psychologists such as Benjamin Martin believe that this accounts for incidences where physical damage to the brain need not affect intelligence at all. By using advanced scanning equipment, however, researchers led by John Duncan of the Cognition and Brain Sciences Unit in Cambridge now think that it is much more localised and at the front of the brain in particular.

Duncan and his team have attempted to link intelligence to the activity of nerve cells in the brain by giving subjects a series of problem solving tests. These tests are of the standard sort used to test and measure intelligence. They resemble puzzles where sequences of numbers or letters have to be rearranged or continued, or patterns of shapes have to be inverted. While subjects are carrying out these intelligence tasks, their heads are scanned to see where electrical activity and blood flow in the brain are concentrated. It turns out that activity was concentrated in the frontal cortex and so, Duncan and his team presume, intelligence is situated there too.

This new idea has not been met with universal acceptance, however. The usual definition of "intelligence" was set by Charles Spearman 100 years ago. This was the quality that allows some people to be very good at a whole variety of things - music, mathematics, practical problem solving and so on - while others are not. He called this quality general intelligence or the "g" factor for short. It was a contentious idea even at the time but still no-one has come up with a better definition. Nonetheless, because the notion of intelligence is imprecisely defined, the idea that there is a fixed location for intelligence has to be questioned.

The questioning comes in an article in the prestigious journal *Science*, the same edition as Duncan's own article. Yale psychologist Robert Sternberg points out that many people who are clearly intelligent, such as leading politicians and lawyers, do very badly in intelligence tests. Conversely, one might argue, there are plenty of academics who are good at intelligence tests but who cannot even tie their own shoe laces! Sternberg implies that the idea that being a successful politician or lawyer does not require intelligence, flies in the face of reason. Rather more likely is the idea that so-called intelligence tests can have little to do with many practical manifestations of intelligence. The skills of verbal and mathematical analysis measured by these tests can tell us very little about the skills of social interaction and people handling which are equally essential for success and are, therefore, equally valid qualities of intelligence.

Sternberg makes a further criticism of the conclusions drawn by Duncan's team. The mental-atlas approach really does not tell us anything about intelligence. The fact that we know a computer's "intelligence" is produced by a computer chip and that we can say where this chip is, does not tell us anything about the computer's intelligence or ability. We could easily move the location of the chip and this would not change the computer's "intelligence". As Benjamin Martin points out, this may be what happens in reality when following physical damage to one area of the brain, knowledge and ability appear able to relocate.

Questions 1 - 8

Classify the following statements as referring to

    A John Duncan   **D** Robert Sternberg
    B Charles Spearman   **E** The writer of the article
    C Benjamin Martin

Write the appropriate letters in boxes 1 - 7 on your answer sheet.

Example	Answer
Physical damage to the brain need not affect intelligence.	C

1 Intelligence can be located throughout the brain.
2 Intelligence makes you good at many different things.
3 Intelligence tests examine limited skills.
4 Intelligence is located at the front of the brain.
5 It is difficult to describe what intelligence is.
6 Intelligence tests can be bad at measuring the intellect of professionals.
7 Intelligence and other abilities can reposition following injury to the brain.
8 Intelligence is a characteristic required by those doing well in legal and political professions.

Questions 9 - 13

Using information contained in the text, complete the following sentences using **NO MORE THAN THREE WORDS** *for each answer.*

9 Spearman's suggested that intelligence was the ability to be good at ....
10 The idea that all politicians and lawyers are unintelligent is ....
11 Spearman's ideas about intelligence are not ....
12 Sternberg suggests that in addition to academic ability, intelligence includes ....
13 Sternberg also believes that intelligence is not affected by where ....

*You should spend about 20 minutes on questions **14 - 27**, which are based on Reading Passage 2 below.*

A New Menace
from an Old Enemy

Malaria is the world's second most common disease causing over 500 million infections and one million deaths every year. Worryingly it is one of those diseases which is beginning to increase as it develops resistance to treatments. Even in the UK, where malaria has been effectively eradicated, more than 2,000 people are infected as they return from trips abroad and the numbers are rising.

It seems as though malaria has been in existence for millions of years and a similar disease may have infected dinosaurs. Malaria-type fevers are recorded among the ancient Greeks by writers such as Herodotus who also records the first prophylactic measures: fishermen sleeping under their own nets. Treatments up until the nineteenth century were as varied as they were ineffective. Live spiders in butter, purging and bleeding, and sleeping with a copy of the Iliad under the patient's head are all recorded. The use of the first genuinely effective remedy, an infusion from the bark of the cinchona tree, was recorded in 1636 but it was only in 1820 that quinine, the active ingredient from the cinchona bark was extracted and modern prevention became possible. For a long time the treatment was regarded with suspicion since it was associated with the Jesuits. Oliver Cromwell, the Protestant English leader who executed King Charles I, died of malaria as a result of his doctors refusing to administer a Catholic remedy! Despite the presence of quinine, malaria was still a major cause of illness and death throughout the nineteenth century. Hundreds of thousands were dying in southern Europe even at the beginning of the last century. Malaria was eradicated from Rome only in the 1930s when Mussolini drained the Pontine marshes.

Despite the fact that malaria has been around for so long, surprisingly little is known about how to cure or prevent it. Mosquitoes, who are the carriers of the disease, are attracted to heat, moisture, lactic acid and carbon dioxide but how they sort through this cocktail to repeatedly select one individual for attention over another is not understood. It is known that the malaria parasite, or *plasmodium falciparum* to give it its Latin name, has a life cycle which must pass through the anopheles mosquito and human hosts in order to live. It can only have attained its present form after mankind mastered agriculture and lived in groups for this to happen. With two such different hosts, the life cycle of the parasite is remarkable.

There is the sporozoite stage which lives in the mosquito. When a human is bitten by an infected anopheles mosquito the parasite is passed to the human through the mosquito's saliva. As few as six such parasites may be enough to pass on the infection provided the human's immune system fails to kill the parasites before they reach the liver. There they transform into merozoites and multiply hugely to, perhaps, about 60,000 after 10 days and then spread throughout the bloodstream. Within minutes of this occurring, they attack the red blood cells to feed on the iron-rich haemoglobin which is inside. This is when the patient begins to feel ill. Within hours they can eat as much as 125 grams of haemoglobin which causes anaemia, lethargy, vulnerability to infection, and oxygen deficiency to areas such as the brain. Oxygen is carried to all organs by haemoglobin in the blood. The lack of oxygen leads to the cells blocking capillaries in the brain and the effects are very much like that of a stroke with one important difference: the damage is reversible and patients can come out of a malarial coma with no brain damage. Merozoites now change into gametocytes which can be male or female and it is this phase, with random mixing of genes that results, that can lead to malaria developing resistance to treatments. These resistant gametocytes, can be passed back to the mosquito if the patient is bitten, and they turn into zygotes. These zygotes divide and produce sporozoites and the cycle can begin again.

The fight against malaria often seems to focus on the work of medical researchers who try to produce solutions such as vaccines. But funding is low because, it is said, malaria is a third world condition and scarcely troubles the rich, industrialised countries. It is true that malaria is, at root, a disease of poverty. The richer countries have managed to eradicate malaria by extending agriculture and so having proper drainage so mosquitoes cannot breed, and by living in solid houses with glass windows so the mosquitoes cannot bite the human host. Campaigns in Hunan province in China, making use of pesticide impregnated netting around beds reduced infection rates from over 1 million per year to around 65,000. But the search for medical cures goes on. Some 15 years ago there were high hopes for DNA based vaccines which worked well in trials on mice. Some still believe that this is where the answer lies and shortly too. Other researchers are not so confident and expect a wait of at least another 15 years before any significant development.

Questions 14 - 21

Do the following statements agree with the information in Reading Passage 2? In boxes 14 - 21 on your answer sheet write **Yes** *if the statement agrees with the information,* **No** *if the statement contradicts the information,* **Not Given** *if there is no information on this in the passage.*

14 Malaria started among the ancient Greeks.
15 Malaria has been eradicated in the wealthier parts of the world.
16 Mosquitoes are discerning in their choice of victims.
17 Treatments in the nineteenth century were ineffective.
18 Iron is a form of nourishment for malarial merizoites.
19 A severe attack of malaria can be similar to a stroke.
20 Research into malaria is not considered a priority by the West.
21 Technological solutions are likely to be more effective than low-tech solutions.

Questions 22 - 27

The diagram below describes the life cycle of the malaria parasite. Complete the spaces with words from the box below. Write your answers in boxes 22 - 27 on your answer sheet. There are more answers than spaces, so you will not use them all.

resistance	zygotes	sporozoites	gametocytes
merozoites	blood	water	saliva

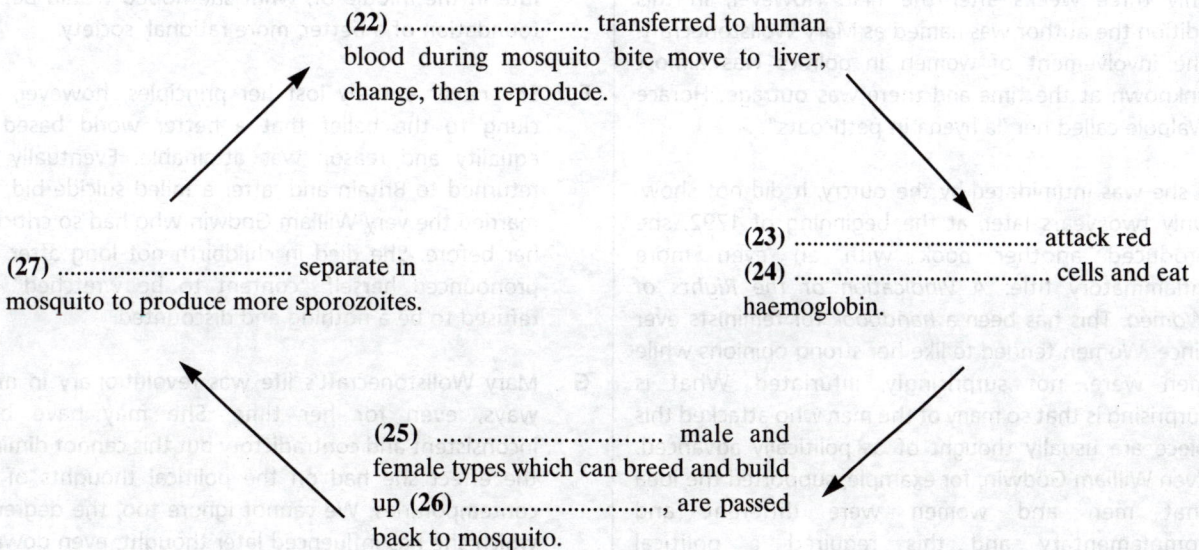

(22) .... transferred to human blood during mosquito bite move to liver, change, then reproduce.

(23) .... attack red
(24) .... cells and eat haemoglobin.

(27) .... separate in mosquito to produce more sporozoites.

(25) .... male and female types which can breed and build up (26) .... , are passed back to mosquito.

Section 3

You should spend about 20 minutes on questions 28 - 40, which are based on Reading Passage 3 below.

Mary Wollstonecraft
——— *The Founder of Feminism* ———

A In 1789 began the celebrated French Revolution, an event which shook the old certainties of European states and European monarchies to the core. It also raised debate on the desired structure of the state throughout whole populations to an unprecedented degree. In October the following year, Edmund Burke brought out his *Reflections on the Revolution in France* which sold 35,000 copies within weeks, then a huge number. It reinforced all the fears and prejudices of the traditional aristocracy. Immediately, more progressive authors began writing their responses including the celebrated Thomas Paine whose *The Rights of Man* sold an amazing two million copies.

B But Paine's was not the first response. Less than a month after Burke's book was published there appeared the anonymous *A Vindication of the Rights of Men*. It sold so well that a second edition appeared only three weeks after the first. However, in this edition the author was named as Mary Wollstonecraft. The involvement of women in politics was almost unknown at the time and there was outrage. Horace Walpole called her "a hyena in petticoats".

C If she was intimidated by the outcry, it did not show. Only two years later, at the beginning of 1792, she produced another book with an even more inflammatory title: *A Vindication of the Rights of Women*. This has been a *handbook* for feminists ever since. Women tended to like her strong opinions while men were, not surprisingly, infuriated. What is surprising is that so many of the men who attacked this piece are usually thought of as politically advanced. Even William Godwin, for example, supported the idea that men and women were different and complementary and this required a political arrangement where men led and women followed. Wollstonecraft attacked this notion and demanded independence and equality for women.

D This rebellious streak led her in quite a different direction from most of her contemporaries. As bloodshed in Paris reached its peak during 1792 and 1793, and most British fled from France, Wollstonecraft moved to Paris to live. She stayed while most of her French friends were killed. Quite why is not clear since she clearly preferred the society of the bourgeois intellectuals who were dying to the street revolutionaries who were killing them. Perhaps it was only after this experience that she appreciated some of the practical pitfalls of unchecked liberty.

E The reality of revolution seemed to change her in a number of other ways. A feature of her *Vindication* was to urge both men and women to subjugate passion to reason. Before her experience in France she had remained single and, single-mindedly, celibate despite the temptation offered by the painter Fuseli. But whilst in France she threw herself into a passionate affair with the American adventurer Gilbert Imlay. She even followed Imlay to Scandinavia in search of stolen silver treasure; a triumph of passion over reason if ever there was one! How ironic that she should suffer this fate in the middle of, what she hoped would be, the foundation of a better, more rational, society.

F She never entirely lost her principles, however, and clung to the belief that a better world based on equality and reason was attainable. Eventually she returned to Britain and, after a failed suicide bid, she married the very William Godwin who had so criticised her before. She died in childbirth not long after and pronounced herself "content to be wretched" but refused to be a nothing and discounted.

G Mary Wollstonecraft's life was revolutionary in many ways, even for her time. She may have been inconsistent and contradictory but this cannot diminish the effect she had on the political thoughts of her contemporaries. We cannot ignore too, the degree to which she has influenced later thought, even down to the present day. Her son-in-law, Percy Shelley, was a fervent admirer who immortalised her in verse in *The Revolt of Islam*. De Beauvoir's *The Second Sex* and Greer's *The Female Eunuch* both owe their origins to Wollstonecraft's pioneering writing. The notions of equality we take for granted today first appeared in her work.

Questions 28 - 33

Reading Passage 3 has seven paragraphs A - G. Choose the most suitable headings for paragraphs A - G from the list of headings below. Write the appropriate i - ix in boxes 28 - 33 on your answer sheet. The first one has been done for you as an example. There are more headings than paragraphs, so you will not use them all.

> Paragraph Headings
>
> | | | | | |
> |---|---|---|---|---|
> | **i)** | A Tragic Ending | **vi)** | Reactions to Revolution |
> | **ii)** | A Revolutionary Life | **vii)** | A Life in Perspective |
> | **iii)** | Being Different | **viii)** | The First Reaction to Burke |
> | **iv)** | Contradictory Behaviour | **ix)** | Asserting the Rights of Women |
> | **v)** | The Work of Thomas Paine | | |

Example	Answer
Paragraph A	vi

28	Paragraph B	....	**31** Paragraph E	....
29	Paragraph C	....	**32** Paragraph F	....
30	Paragraph D	....	**33** Paragraph G	....

Questions 34 - 40

*Choose the appropriate answers **A - D** and write them in boxes 34 - 40 on your answer sheet.*

34 The revolution in France
   A frightened everybody.
   B prejudiced the aristocracy.
   C concerned everybody.
   D challenged the established order.

35 Wollstonecraft's *A Vindication of the Rights of Men*
   A was an immediate best seller.
   B sold only slowly at first.
   C hardly sold at all.
   D was only read by women.

36 The response to *A Vindicaton of the Rights of Men*
   A intimidated Mary.
   B made Mary flee to France.
   C attracted William Godwin.
   D made Mary write another book.

37 Men objected to the book because

A it was written by a woman.

B it challenged established ideas about men and women.

C she published before them.

D the writer was a female politician.

38 Mary's personal life

A always matched her published beliefs.

B sometimes contradicted her published beliefs.

C never contradicted her published beliefs.

D never matched her published beliefs.

39 In refusing to be discounted she meant

A women should be taught literacy and numeracy.

B the role of women should not be reduced.

C she was not to be overlooked for being a woman.

D she was happy as she was.

40 Mary Wollstonecraft's writing

A was constant and contemporary.

B inspired modern feminist writers.

C took equality for granted.

D was ignored.

ACADEMIC WRITING
PRACTICE TEST 4

1 hour

WRITING TASK 1

You should spend about 20 minutes on this task.

The following graph gives information about book-buying over 30 years in New York.

Write a report for a university lecturer describing the information shown below.

You should write at least 150 words.

1: average number of books bought per person per year

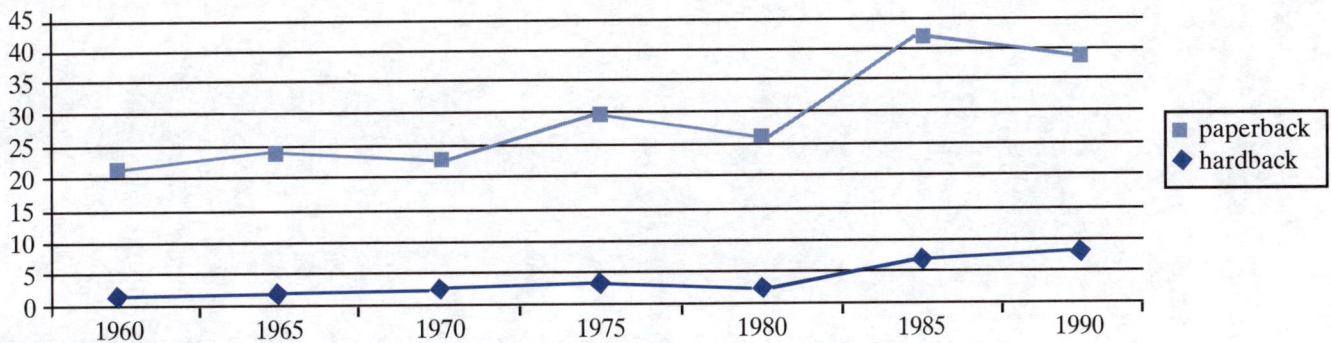

2: types of books bought per person per year

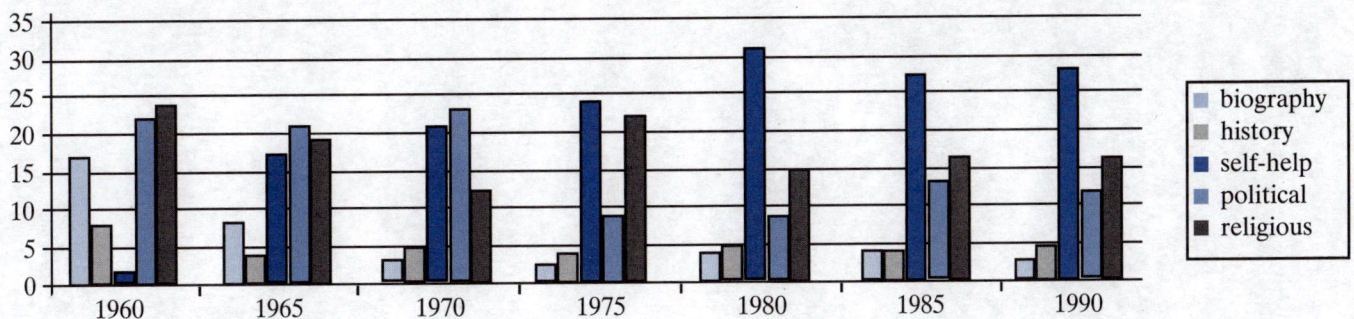

WRITING TASK 2

You should spend about 40 minutes on this task.

Present a written argument or case to an educated reader with no specialist knowledge of the following topic.

Sports which depend on violence for their entertainment, such as boxing and wrestling, have no place in a civilised society and should be banned.

To what extent would you support or reject this idea?

You should write at least 250 words.

You should use your own ideas, knowledge and experience and support your arguments with examples and relevant evidence.

SPEAKING
PRACTICE TEST 4

Part 1

I'd like you to tell me something about where you live. Is that okay?

- What sort of place do you come from? Is it a city, a town or a village?
- Have your family always lived there?
- What work do people in your community do?
- Do you think it is a nice place to live in? Why? Why not?
- What changes have you seen there?

Part 2

Describe a sport, hobby or other pastime you are particularly interested in.

You should say:
- how you started this activity.
- how the activity works.
- whether you need any special equipment.
- what benefits can be obtained from this activity

- How would you persuade someone to take up this hobby/sport/pastime?
- What leisure activities are most popular in your country?

Part 3

- sports
  - Describe the most popular sports in your country.
  - Compare modern pastimes with traditional ones.
  - Evaluate the advantages and disadvantages of competitive sports.

- hobbies and pastime
  - Describe the traditional hobbies and pastimes in your country.
  - Discuss the view that computer games are changing hobbies and games in your society.

- television
  - Describe your television viewing habits.
  - Discuss whether television is harmful for young people.
  - Assess the quality of TV programmes in your country.

GENERAL TRAINING
PAPERS

GENERAL TRAINING READING

PRACTICE TEST 1

NUMBER OF QUESTIONS: 40
TIME PERMITTED: 1 HOUR

Instructions

WRITE ALL ANSWERS ON THE ANSWER SHEET

The test is organised as follows:

Reading Passage 1	*Questions 1 - 13*
Reading Passage 2	*Questions 14 - 27*
Reading Passage 3	*Questions 28 - 40*

Start at the beginning of the test and read the passages in order. Answer all the questions. If you are not sure of an answer, you can leave it and try to answer it later.

Section 1 Questions 1 - 13

Questions 1 - 6

For Questions 1 - 6, read the statements below, the extracts about East Deane College and the application form. In boxes 1 - 6 on your answer sheet write **Yes** *if the statement is true,* **No** *if the statement is false and* **Not Given** *if the information is not given in the passage.*

Example	Answer
East Deane College receives money from the Martin John Trust.	Yes

1 Mr Jones is an expert at making musical instruments.
2 Ronald Carter teaches furniture making.
3 East Deane College provides qualifications in architectural glass work.
4 The College provides all necessary materials.
5 Mr Jones wants to live in the College during the course.
6 Mr Jones is employed.

East Deane College

East Deane is a private educational foundation funded through the Martin John Trust. It provides intensive vocational training in the traditional crafts of musical instrument making, tapestry design and weaving, and architectural glass and metal work. It also provides a series of shorter weekend and holiday courses for the enthusiastic amateur in various crafts, taking advantage of the superb facilities offered by East Deane.

Courses in Woodwork

21 - 23 April	Rustic Furniture Making	(Eric Machin)
27 - 30 April	Turning for Beginners	(Ronald Carter)
4 - 6 May	Advanced Turning	(Ronald Carter)
10 - 18 May	Musical Instrument Making Course (apply for special brochure)	
22 - 24 May	Picture Framing	(Martin MacCarthy)
28 - 30 May	Freehand Carving	(Jean Atkinson)

Musical Instrument Making Course
(Joan Juliard, R Z Smith and Gordon Smith)

Course fee: £628 (concessions for OAPs, students and unemployed)

This 9-day course will allow interested woodworkers to plan and make a complete musical instrument during the course of their stay, no matter what the level of their woodworking abilities.

Beginner Level
Appalachian Dulcimer, Renaissance Flute

Intermediate Level
Modern Guitar, Violin, Bagpipes

Advanced Woodworkers
Renaissance Guitar, Bass Viol

Students are asked to bring their own woodworking tools (and to mark these clearly), although a full range of power and other tools will be available. Wood for the instruments must be bought separately from tutors.

The course is fully-catered but students must indicate if they wish to live in College accommodation during the course. This can be indicated on the application form.

Musical Instrument Making Course
Application Form

Name   *Brian Jones*   Address   *6 The Elms*
                                                      Stanton
Date of Birth   *5th March 1945*   *Portsmouth PO2 4EQ*

What instrument do you want to make?
1st choice   *Appalachian Dulcimer*
2nd choice   *Renaissance Flute*

Accommodation
single room   *Yes*   double room   none
(If you choose a double room, please indicate with whom you will be sharing)

Fee Paid (please enclose a cheque for the appropriate amount) *£628*

Questions 7 - 13

Using **NO MORE THAN THREE WORDS** *answer the following questions. Write your answers in boxes 7 - 13 on your answer sheet.*

7   When does Mr Jones have to pay for his accommodation?
8   Mr Jones is unsure where and when dinner is provided. Who should he contact?
9   Another student breaks a mirror in Mr Jones' room during a party. Who pays?
10 Why might Mr Jones be disturbed while sleeping?
11 When do guests have to vacate their rooms?
12 If Mr Jones wants help with his suitcases, which room should he go to?
13 If Mr Jones needs a receipt, where should he go?

East Deane College
Accommodation Information and Agreement

Almost all rooms are single and with their own bathrooms. A small number of double rooms are available and these will be allocated strictly on a first come, first served basis. For temporary students who want to live in the College during their course, an application form must be completed. Signing and returning this form indicates agreement to the terms and conditions listed below.

1 Payment for accommodation must be made in full and in advance.
2 The College accepts that reasonable wear and tear will occur but damage beyond this is the sole responsibility of the occupant of the room, who must pay in full.
3 Guests may check in anytime after midday on the day of enrolment and must check out before 10 am on their day of departure.
4 Guests are expected to make themselves acquainted with the fire instructions and the location of the fire exit nearest to their room. (Practice fire drills may be carried out at night.)

Useful names and numbers

Enquiries about charges:	Mrs Robertson, room 21
Other enquiries:	Miss Smith, room 22
Porter:	Mr Ferguson, room 06
Complaints:	The Duty Manager, room 01

Section 2

*You should spend about 20 minutes on questions **14 - 26**, which are based on Reading Passage 2 below.*

Personnel Development in Jago International Ltd

A Jago International is a by-word for quality in vocational education. From training in the use of the humble word processor to the highest level of negotiation skills, Jago International will arrange for employers to gain the most from their employees' abilities, and for employees to make the best of themselves. Jago International has an unblemished record of achievement after more than 50 years' work with the world's largest companies.

B Jago International is committed to the personal and professional development of its own staff. This is in keeping with its philosophy of 'Achieving the best, for the best of all possible worlds'. Only if our own staff are fully-trained and fulfilled can our customers receive the most up-to-date and most effective training for their own development.

C Staff are encouraged to pursue both personal and professional qualifications to ensure they fulfil their potential to the greatest degree. There are a number of ways staff can achieve this with the support of Jago International. Staff may take any of the wide assortment of training courses administered through our own Professional Development Unit. Staff may be directed to take outside qualifications from other training providers where we do not provide these qualifications ourselves. Staff may also wish to take time to pursue individual training goals and, where appropriate, Jago International will support this.

D Jago International's Professional Development Unit is housed in our Freemantle headquarters but delivers courses on-site in each of our regional centres. A monthly schedule of courses available is sent to every section and department head and is posted on main notice boards and the Jago website. These courses extend from word processing and spreadsheet use, to staff and project management, to our own MBA courses run in association with the University of Freemantle. These courses are free to all Jago staff. Applications should be made through your line supervisor or head of department.

E It may be appropriate to take courses or qualifications which are not covered in the range offered by our PDU. Staff are encouraged to take courses and qualifications with other training organisations with the agreement of their line supervisor or head of department. Support and funding is available to staff through the PDU where this is thought appropriate and helpful to the company as a whole. Application forms for funding can be obtained from Dr Bob Morley, the Director of our PDU, but must be submitted by the appropriate head of department. Within the last year we have supported staff taking courses in Advanced Marketing at the University of Freemantle. It is company policy for staff to make some financial commitment to the courses they take in these circumstances.

F Staff may also wish to take other courses or training for their own personal development and there are opportunities for support here too. The PDU has a budget for extraordinary training to provide some help to staff undertaking training in this category. This is also administered by Dr Morley in the PDU and an application form should be sought from him. Currently being funded are courses at the Queensland Higher College in aromatherapy and spiritual cleansing.

G For a full description of all courses and funding opportunities available to staff through Jago International, contact Dr Bob Morley on extension 5391 or at the Professional Development Unit at the Headquarters Building.

Questions 14 - 19

Read the article on page 68 which has seven paragraphs A - G. Choose the most suitable headings for paragraphs B - F from the list of headings below. Write the appropriate numbers i - x in boxes 14 - 19 on your answer sheet. The first one has been done for you as an example. There are more headings than paragraphs, so you will not use them all.

List of Headings

i)	About Jago International	**vi)**	The Professional Development Unit
ii)	Training Outside Jago	**vii)**	Find out More
iii)	Jago's Training Worldwide	**viii)**	Routes to Professional Development
iv)	Personal Development	**ix)**	Why Jago Encourages Personnel Development
v)	Achieving the Best	**x)**	Queensland Higher College

Example	Answer
Paragraph A	i

14	Paragraph B	....	**17**	Paragraph E	....
15	Paragraph C	....	**18**	Paragraph F	....
16	Paragraph D	....	**19**	Paragraph G	....

Questions 20 - 26

For questions 20 - 26, complete the summary below using the best word or expression from those provided in the box. Write your answers in the boxes 20 - 26 on the answer sheet.

might	routes	with	works	by	encourages	specialises
time	want	ways	money	will	suggested	recommended

Jago International is a company which .... **(20)** in providing training in other companies. It has been going for more than 50 years. Jago .... **(21)** its own staff to undergo training. It provides three different .... **(22)** to training. Firstly, staff can take training at its own Professional Development Unit, although some courses are run .... **(23)** the University of Freemantle. These courses are free. Secondly, staff can be .... **(24)** to take courses outside the Professional Development Unit. Staff must contribute some of their own .... **(25)** to these courses. Finally, staff can take any other course which interests them and Jago .... **(26)** offer some financial help.

Section 3

Questions 27 - 40
Read the following passage and answer questions 27 to 40.

International Day: is it good or bad for the city?

Expenditure by shop type (£000)

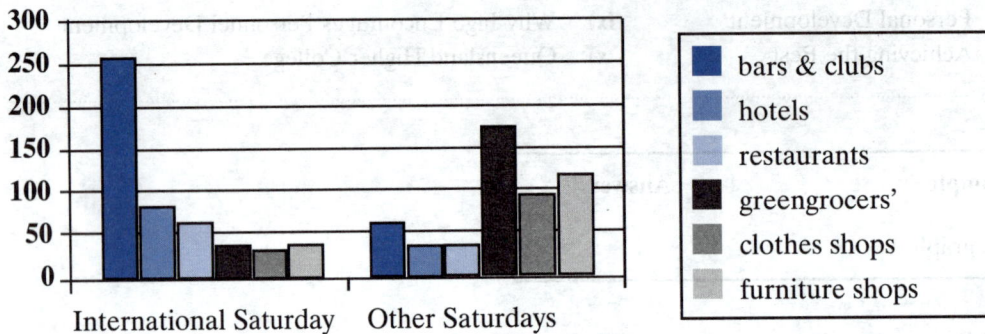

Legend:
- bars & clubs
- hotels
- restaurants
- greengrocers'
- clothes shops
- furniture shops

International Saturday   Other Saturdays

Everyone loves International Day in Wellington. International rugby is part of New Zealand's culture and besides, a big international match with the All Blacks playing Australia or South Africa is good for the local economy. Thousands of rugby fans bring money into the city when they come to the match and we all benefit from this boost to the local economy. That is the theory. So why do so many local retailers hate International Day? Is it as good for the economy as we are led to believe?

Superficially, it is easy to see how money enters the local economy from this source. The sale of tickets for the international match alone raises nearly $5 million and the sale of television rights a further $2 million. Part of this is used to employ match stewards and ticket collectors at the game. Rugby supporters from overseas need to stay in hotels and they need to eat so they spend money in hotels and restaurants. All rugby fans, both home and away, like a drink and the bars and clubs do an excellent trade. It is estimated that rugby fans may spend $250,000 on drinks and a further $75,000 on hotels and accommodation over an international weekend. Some of this information can be seen on the graph.

So where is the problem? The assumption here is that all this extra money, over $7 million, is additional to the money in the local economy. There are two reasons for thinking this may be a wrong assumption. One is that a good deal of this money may not stay local - it is, in fact, spent elsewhere or even in another country. The second is the possibility that this particular form of trade will drive out existing trade and may depress the local economy.

Let us look at the first of these possibilities and look specifically at the revenue from the game itself. Money from television rights is something that never sees the local economy at all. The International Rugby Board negotiates the $2 million deal and takes the fee. The New Zealand Rugby Union will get a portion of this, about 4.5%, which it will use to foster the game at a national level. Specialist cameramen, technicians and commentators may well fly in from abroad to cover the game and then fly out again afterwards, taking their fees with them. The money from ticket sales is likewise widely distributed. Only 20% of the total is paid to the Wellington National Rugby Ground to cover the hire of the stadium and the cost of match day staff. The remaining 80% is split evenly between the competing rugby unions. The unions will give approximately 5% of this back to the Wellington Rugby Club, who provide the union with so many of its players. So it would seem that only a quarter of the money from ticket sales would stay in the local economy. This is significantly less than would appear at first.

There is an argument too that international rugby may actually drive certain money out of the economy. A look at the graph shows that certain shops and trades, far from carrying out good trade on International Day, suffer a significant slump. Shops which sell unprepared foodstuffs or clothes, for example, see their trade cut by a half or even three quarters when rugby comes to town. It would seem that, rather than face a city full of exuberant rugby fans, many potential customers will go elsewhere to shop. Every match day greengrocers lose A$100,000, clothes and furniture sellers a further $A70,000 each. There are many other retailers in this category. Even the bars and restaurants lose their regular trade over rugby weekends. $250,000 of new drinking income may come into the bars but the usual $50,000 of trade appears to stay at home and the evidence shows that it does not immediately return the following weekend.

This study is far from complete but it does provide persuasive evidence that international rugby does not only bring money into Wellington, it also drives it out, perhaps in equal measure. Add to the equation the extra cost of policing and clearing up after 100,000 visitors to the city centre and Wellington may actually be paying for the privilege of hosting internationals. But then, most rugby fans would willingly do that anyway!

Questions 27 - 30

Use the figures and expressions in the box to answer the following questions. Write your answers in boxes 27 - 30 on your answer sheet.

nearly $5 million	about $1 million	about $250,000	about $140,000
over $7 million	about $200,000	about $325,000	

27 How much money does an international rugby match appear to bring to Wellington?
28 How much is spent on hotels and drinks?
29 How much money does the Wellington National Rugby Ground get from ticket sales?
30 How much money do clothes and furniture shops combined lose over an international weekend?

Questions 31 - 35

Below is a list of shops and other businesses in Wellington. Say whether these businesses gain money or lose money over an international weekend. In boxes 31 - 35 on your answer sheet write **G** *if they gain money,* **L** *if they lose money,* **NG** *if information for this is not given in the passage.*

31 bars
32 restaurants
33 greengrocers
34 the New Zealand Rugby Union
35 Wellington City Council

Questions 36 - 40

Complete the sentences below using **NO MORE THAN THREE WORDS** *for each answer. Write your answers in boxes 36 - 40 on your answer sheet.*

36 It is commonly believed that the income from international rugby enhances ....
37 After paying for the ground, the rival rugby unions divide the proceeds from the ticket sales ....
....
38 Stores trading in non-edible merchandise have their business ....
39 Wellington Council must pay for additional ....
40 The businesses which benefit most are the ....

GENERAL TRAINING READING

PRACTICE TEST 2

NUMBER OF QUESTIONS: 40
TIME PERMITTED: 1 HOUR

Instructions

WRITE ALL ANSWERS ON THE ANSWER SHEET

The test is organised as follows:

Reading Passage 1	Questions 1 - 14
Reading Passage 2	Questions 15 - 27
Reading Passage 3	Questions 28 - 40

Start at the beginning of the test and read the passages in order. Answer all the questions. If you are not sure of an answer, you can leave it and try to answer it later.

Section 1 Questions 1 - 14

Questions 1 - 6

Look at the descriptions of residential accommodation available to students at Brick Lane College. Each description is labelled A - F. Use these letters to answer questions 1 - 6 about these descriptions. An example has been done for you. Write your answers in boxes 1 - 6 on your answer sheet.

Example	Answer
Which accommodation used to belong to a noble?	A

1 Which accommodation is intended for students with families?
2 Which accommodation offers some meals but not all?
3 Which accommodation is located in an area which is full of life?
4 Which accommodation is best for learning English?
5 In which accommodation must you cook for yourself?
6 Which accommodation would be suitable for some close friends who want to live together?

Brick Lane College
Residential Accommodation

A Blane Castle	**B** Buck Hall
This mock Gothic castle was the family home of Lord Whitehouse before becoming a college residence in 1978. It offers large, luxury rooms with beautiful views over the Thames Estuary. • double rooms available • choice of fully-catered or self-catering • easy walk or 5-minute bus ride to College campus Cost: £58 per week self-catering £98 per week fully-catered	Buck Hall is a row of Victorian terraced houses converted to halls of residence in 1965. Situated in the lively suburb of Lowlands. Small but thoroughly modern rooms with own bathrooms. • 10-minute walk to College • fully-catered • wide range of pubs, clubs and supermarkets in easy reach Cost: £47 per week
C Susan Hayhoe Hall	**D** Danver House
Modern tower block purpose-built as a hall of residence in 1968 and situated on the Brick Lane main campus. • bed and breakfast only • wide range of cafés and restaurants on campus • many rooms with bathrooms • double rooms available Cost: £39 per week	Former mansion which is now a house shared by students. Near the campus. • 8 shared bedrooms • shared bathroom and kitchen • shared dining room and lounge • porter and security provided Cost: £41 per week
E Family Homes	**F** Whitehouse Flats
A range of accommodation is available with host families. Especially recommended for students from overseas who need help with their language. • individual study-bedroom • friendly conversation guaranteed • bed, breakfast and other meals provided • lunch provided by arrangement • all within 5-minute bus ride of College Cost: £89 per week	2, 3 and 4 bedroom flats available in block of flats beautifully situated in a park overlooking the sea. Car may be required. • fully furnished • own kitchen and bathroom • car park facilities available • bus service to College • all windows and doors are childproof Cost: £101 - 151 per week per flat

Questions 7 - 14

Now read this letter from Marilyn who will become a student at Brick Lane College next year. Complete the application form using **NO MORE THAN THREE WORDS** *for each answer. Write your answers in boxes 7 - 14 on your answer sheet.*

Dear Mandy

Many thanks for your "Get Well" card and the lovely flowers. They really cheered me up while I was in hospital. But I'm out and well on the mend. The doctors were very kind and refused to believe I'll be 30 next birthday and said I was recuperating as if I was only 18. I'll be on crutches for a few weeks but after that I'll be back to normal - well in time for starting college. I'll be more careful the next time I go skiing!

Talking of college, I've got the details of the accommodation and I need to make up my mind about where and what type to go for. I think I'd like to be with other students from outside the History department. It's easier to make friends in Physics or Drama or something that way, so I think staying with a family is out of the question. And I don't want to share a bathroom - silly I know - so I guess I'll have to pay a bit more if I want my own. I suppose that rules out Danver House, which is a pity because otherwise it seemed nice. I'd consider it if I couldn't find a cheap room with a bathroom. It's got to be close to college because I don't have a car and I don't think I can afford the bus. And it has to be as cheap as possible - the views of the estuary from Blane Castle sound lovely but it is rather pricey.

I'm not fond of institution food so I'd prefer somewhere I can do most of the cooking myself. Perhaps having breakfast prepared for me wouldn't be so bad. Not even the college cooks can ruin coffee and toast, surely! So you've probably worked out I'll try to stay on campus for my first choice and for my second I'd share with you if you and your friends are still willing. I'd just have to put up with sharing the bathroom so I could stay with other students, I suppose. Not ideal but you can't have everything.

What do you think? You'd better give me a call soon because I need to send off this form by the end of the week.

Lots of Love

Marilyn

Brick Lane College Accommodation Application Form	
Surname	Brown
Forenames	**(7)**
Department you have been accepted for	**(8)**
Age	**(9)**
Type of accommodation requested:	
1st choice	**(10)**
2nd choice	**(11)**
Do you want your own bathroom? (write N/A if not applicable)	**(12)**
Would you be prepared to share a room?	**(13)**
If so, who with?	**(14)**
What form of catering do you want?	**N/A**
For non self-catering students, do you have any special requirements?	**N/A**
Do you have any disability we should know about?	**No**

Section 2 | **Questions 15 - 27**

Questions 15 - 22
For questions 15 - 22 read the passage below.

The Academic English Course
Harold Wood and Mark Stey

These course books are designed for students taking Foundation level courses in college or university and who are preparing to study other subjects to degree level at English speaking institutions. They are designed to raise students' levels of general English and enhance their academic study skills in English.

This course consists of:
1 Academic Starter English
2 Academic English for Study

Academic Starter English

Academic Starter English is designed for intermediate level students or for students returning to study after a period away from the English language. It is designed to bring learners up to the level where they can read and understand academic style English quickly and easily, and to the level where they can write accurately in English. The course is based on extensive research on the problems faced by non-native speakers studying in Australia and covers not only structural and functional elements of the language but also focuses on problem and error correction. Learners' main problems and fears are directly addressed and dealt with.

The course is divided into six units:
- reading faster and reading better
- using English tenses
- write the right way
- listen well
- say what you mean
- curing common mistakes

Each unit contains extensive notes and explanations for student use, together with role play and exercises to practise the elements of language being taught. There are tapes and videos to accompany the course book and a complete teacher's book with answers and recommendations on how to handle and teach the materials. A CD-Rom is also available for additional practice. Homework and other tasks for assessment are included. The Starter course is designed to last for 1 semester or about 50 contact hours of classes.

Academic English for Study

Academic English for Study is designed for students who are upper-intermediate level and will give them the academic study skills they need to succeed in taking a degree through the medium of English. The course will focus on the vocabulary and structures of academic-style English and the four skill areas. Use is made of the research carried out by Professor Paul Nation on the structure and content of Academic English. By the end of the course a successful student may not be perfect in English but should be able to function easily alongside native speakers.

The course is divided into six units:
- the words you need
- academic style and structure
- reading academic texts
- writing in the appropriate style
- taking notes from lectures
- making academic presentations

Each unit contains explanations and practice materials as well as exercises for homework or assessment. There is a teacher's book with model answers and explanations. There is a set of five tapes to accompany the course. The Study course is designed to last for 1 semester or about 50 contact hours of classes.

Questions 15 - 22

Read the passage about the English courses and look at the statements below. In boxes 15 - 22 on your answer sheet write **True** *if the statement is true,* **False** *if the statement is false,* **Not Given** *if the information is not given in the passage.*

15   Beginners can use this course.

16   The Starter course will help learners to speak.

17   The Starter course corrects frequently occurring mistakes.

18   The course will measure your ability in English.

19   The Academic course lasts for a year.

20   After the course learners will be as good as native speakers of English.

21   The teacher's books both contain notes on how to teach.

22   The book is based on Harold Wood and Mark Stey's research.

Questions 23 - 27

For questions 23 - 27 read the passage below.

Review of *The Academic English Course* by Harold Wood and Mark Stey

English for Academic Purposes is big business. Every year hundreds of thousands of learners embark on courses in the hope of getting the right abilities and qualifications to take a degree in Britain, Australia, New Zealand or the USA. There is a huge number of course books designed principally, one suspects, to raise money for the writers rather than tackle the lengthy and difficult business of training students to study properly and appropriately. How refreshing, then, to try out *The Academic English Course* by Harold Wood and Mark Stey, which does exactly what it should do. Other courses may be like over-expensive and underpowered 4x4s but this is a real Rolls Royce, with every part carefully honed and expensive but worth the money. It is a course which will appeal to teachers rather than the pupils, since it is the teacher's institutions who will use it as a course book. It is well-organised and thorough and clearly based on a wealth of practical experience by the writers. I found I didn't need to prepare extensively with this course since it was all so clear and well-organised. It deserves to do well and I will be disappointed, and surprised, if it does not become the best seller it deserves to be.

Using **NO MORE THAN THREE WORDS** *answer the following questions. Write your answers in boxes 23 - 27 on your answer sheet.*

23   Why does the writer think most authors write course books? ....

24   What does the writer think the book teaches the students to do? ....

25   What is the writer's opinion of the book? ....

26   Who does the writer think will be the main buyers of the book? ....

27   What does the writer hope the book will be? ....

Section 3 | Questions 28 - 40

Questions 28 - 34

Read the article on page 80 which has eight paragraphs A - H. Choose the most suitable headings for paragraphs B - H from the list of headings below. Write the appropriate numbers i - x in boxes 28 - 34 on your answer sheet. The first one has been done for you as an example. There are more headings than paragraphs, so you will not use them all.

List of Headings

i)	A Major Tourist Attraction	vi)	A Hazardous Occupation
ii)	Catering for Special Needs	vii)	The Legacy of Mining
iii)	Visiting Times	viii)	The Pit's Contribution to Australia
iv)	From Homestead to Mine	ix)	Darling Pit's Facilities
v)	Mining Disasters	x)	Darling Pit Today

Example	Answer
Paragraph A	viii

28	Paragraph B	....	32	Paragraph F	....
29	Paragraph C	....	33	Paragraph G	....
30	Paragraph D	....	34	Paragraph H	....
31	Paragraph E	....			

The Darling Pit

A Situated in the Great Barrier Mountains, near the headwaters of the Darling River, is one of Australia's earliest industrial monuments: the Darling Pit. Darling Pit is the mine that started industrial development in Australia providing coal
- to power the factories
- to help run ships and the railways
- to make steel
- to heat homes

B Begun in 1809 on Paul Darling's farmstead when resources of coal and iron were found near the surface, the Darling Pit was rapidly transformed from a simple drift mine into the world's biggest, and deepest, coal mine. 94 miles of tunnels extending up to 600 feet below ground were all dug by hand. At its height in 1850, over 15,000 men were employed in the pit and it produced over 1.5 million tons of coal annually. It continued as a working mine until 1978 and is now preserved as a museum and a monument to the men who worked here.

C A glance from the surrounding hillside as you approach the Darling Pit will show you how mining transformed the local scenery as well as the local economy. The Darling Pit retains its nineteenth century ironworks, pit head machinery, 3,000 terraced houses built to accommodate the work-force, a chapel and 4 pubs. Even the original farmhouse survives. This tight-knit community is now surrounded by slag heaps; the mountains of soil and other waste dug out to get to the coal.

D Mining was a dangerous occupation in the nineteenth century. Most mines suffered deaths from tunnel collapse and from flooding. Pneumoconiosis, an inflammation of the lungs brought about by prolonged exposure to coal dust, was also a common problem and historical works from the last century refer to the ease of identifying ex-miners by the Darling cough. The major problem in the Darling mine, however, was the prevalence of inflammable coal gas in the area, which resulted in the underground explosions of 1854 and 1910. Monuments to the 485 miners who died in these tragedies can be seen in the chapel.

E The Darling Pit is still a real colliery, even though it no longer produces coal. There is still a staff of over 100 who maintain the mine and assist the visitors. The Pit now allows tourists and visitors to undertake guided tours of the works, including a tour of selected shafts underground. Many of the guides are ex-miners who will explain the workings of the mine and tell you many stories from their personal experience. Helmets, lamps and protective clothing are provided, although visitors are reminded that it can be cold underground and they are advised to wear something warm as well as sensible protective footwear.

F The Darling Pit now has all the amenities needed for a major tourist attraction. Many of the buildings on the surface are open for exploration: the engine house at the pit head, the blacksmith's shop, the pit head baths and the stables (remember pit ponies provided much of the power for moving coal before the electric engine became available). The miners' pubs now feature as canteens and restaurants, offering a range of fast and high quality food and drink. There are picnic areas, toilets, a gift shop and even a photographic studio. The miners' chapel is also available for those who would like to spend time in quiet contemplation or prayer.

G It is regretted that children under 5 cannot be taken on tours underground, although they can visit all the surface exhibits. Visitors in wheelchairs can be accommodated, even underground, but please notify the ticket office of this on entry.

H Opening hours are 9.30 am to 5.00 pm daily in summer from the beginning of April to the end of September. During winter opening is from 10.00 am to 4.00 pm. The site is open every day including weekends and bank holidays except for Christmas Day. Please note, however, that the underground section of the Pit may be closed for maintenance during the winter and visitors should ring in advance to avoid disappointment. Underground tours start from 10.00 am in the summer and 11.00 am in winter and last admissions are at 3.30 pm throughout the year. A complete tour will take at least 3 hours and could last all day. Group rates are available, as are concessions for school parties and OAPs. There is a free car park.

Questions 35 - 40

Choose the appropriate letters A - D and write them in boxes 35 - 40 on your answer sheet.

35 The Darling Pit was originally
A a factory.
B a mine.
C a farm.
D a house.

36 Mining in the Darling Pit was particularly dangerous because of
A tunnel collapse.
B pneumoconiosis.
C flooding.
D coal gas.

37 You should check with the pit before visiting in winter because
A it opens later.
B it closes for maintenance.
C it closes earlier.
D notice is needed for wheelchair visitors.

38 During summer tours start at
A 9.30 am.
B 10.00 am.
C 11.00 am.
D 3.30 pm.

39 Children under 5 cannot go to
A the slag heaps.
B the area below ground.
C the blacksmith's shop.
D the stables.

40 The Darling Pit now employs
A more than 100 people.
B 3,000 people.
C 15,000 people.
D 1.5 million people.

WRITING TASK 1

You should spend about 20 minutes on this task.

You wrote to the Harvey School of English last month asking for a brochure and for details of how to arrange accommodation. You have received nothing. You have telephoned but only spoken to the caretaker.

Write a letter to the school owners. Explain the situation and tell them what you want to happen.

You should write at least 150 words.

You do NOT need to write your own address.

Begin the letter as follows:

Dear Sir/Madam,

WRITING TASK 2

You should spend about 40 minutes on this task.

Your local newspaper asks you to prepare a short article for them on the following topic.

Many governments are now trying to prevent global warming and the effect it has on our environment. They are trying to reduce the things which contribute to global warming such as pollution from cars and destruction of the rain forests.

Describe what you think the problem is and the actions you think your government should take to solve it.

You should write at least 250 words. You need not include a headline.

1 hour

WRITING TASK 1

You should spend about 20 minutes on this task.

You have bought a packet of breakfast cereal at Gibbon's Supermarket. When you opened it at home it had clearly gone bad.

Write a letter of complaint to the manager of the supermarket and explain what you want to happen.

You should write at least 150 words.

You do NOT need to write your own address.

Begin the letter as follows:

Dear Sir/Madam,

WRITING TASK 2

You should spend about 40 minutes on this task.

As part of a school assignment you have to write about the following topics.

Schools and parents often require their pupils to wear school uniforms. The pupils, however, usually dislike this. There are acceptable arguments both for and against the wearing of school uniforms.

Explain some of the arguments both for and against the wearing of school uniforms and state what is your opinion on the subject.

You should write at least 250 words.

ANSWER SHEET

In the Reading and Listening examinations candidates are expected to record their answers on an answer sheet. In the Listening examination extra time is provided for this.

In the real examination these answer sheets are also used to record information about the candidate, the centre and the exam versions being taken. Below this is the section where candidates record their answers.

Below is an example of the answer sheet. You may copy this and use it to practise writing your answers.

	Answers	Mark	
1		☐	☐
2		☐	☐
3		☐	☐
4		☐	☐
5		☐	☐
6		☐	☐
7		☐	☐
8		☐	☐
9		☐	☐
10		☐	☐
11		☐	☐
12		☐	☐
13		☐	☐
14		☐	☐
15		☐	☐
16		☐	☐
17		☐	☐
18		☐	☐
19		☐	☐
20		☐	☐

	Answers	Mark	
21		☐	☐
22		☐	☐
23		☐	☐
24		☐	☐
25		☐	☐
26		☐	☐
27		☐	☐
28		☐	☐
29		☐	☐
30		☐	☐
31		☐	☐
32		☐	☐
33		☐	☐
34		☐	☐
35		☐	☐
36		☐	☐
37		☐	☐
38		☐	☐
39		☐	☐
40		☐	☐

Listening Test 1

*You will hear a number of different recordings and you have to answer questions on what you hear. There will be time for you to read the instructions and you will have a chance to check your answers. The recordings will be heard only **once**. The test is in four sections. Record all your answers in your test book and at the end of the test you will be given 10 minutes to transfer your answers to a special answer sheet.*

Now turn to Section 1.

Section 1

You will hear a policeman giving a talk to some students. First you will have some time to look at questions 1 to 6 (pause for 30 seconds).

You will see that there has been an example written for you. On this occasion only the conversation relating to the example will be played first (listen to example being played).

*Sergeant Brown is going to speak about safety so answer **b** has been circled on the question page.*

Now we will begin. You should answer the questions as you listen as you will not hear the recording a second time. Listen to the talk carefully and answer questions 1 to 6.

[man] ... and so I'd like to hand you over now to Sergeant Brown. Thank you.

[2nd man]
Thank you, Mr Fogarty. Er, yes, as you know my name is Sergeant Jeff Brown, and as Mr Fogarty has indicated, I'll be speaking to you briefly today about security, about how to make your time at this university safer and more comfortable. I am officially the university liaison officer, which means I have a specific brief to act as a go-between for the university and the police, if there are problems, and also to offer an official presence on or around campus and give individuals advice if they need it.

Now, my job is very important to me. I take security and reducing the threat of crime on this campus very seriously, because although I don't actually live on the campus, both my daughters attended this university, and my son is still here. So I am a local policeman in every respect. I have been the university liaison officer for the last five years but I have been in the police force for 15 in all.

Now, on to some advice. The first thing I want to stress is that this university is a comparatively safe place to live. We have had no serious crimes here in the five years I've been here. In fact, crime of any sort is very rare on the campus. We have good security here and although there are a lot of staff and students, the security staff, including myself, make an effort to get to know your faces!

However, as students it is of course wise for you to take precautions to protect yourselves against crime when you are off the campus. As I said, the campus itself is really very safe, but there is a large park right behind it, MacGowen Fields, and although this is a beautiful place to sit or walk during the day, at night you must be careful. One or two students have reported unpleasant incidents at night while walking in the park, although it must be said that no major incidents have been reported.

Now, there are no areas in town which I advise students to avoid as a general rule, but the town centre is more hazardous than other areas, especially in the evenings on Friday and Saturday. On these days there is often fighting after people have had too much to drink in the pubs and clubs in the area. There have also been a number of robberies and muggings.

Before the talk continues you have some time to read questions 7 to 10 (pause for 20 seconds). Now listen carefully and answer questions 7 to 10.

Well, that was my advice to you. Most of it is common sense but remember crime always happens when you least expect it. But there are ways to protect yourself. First of all, the university provides all students with personal alarms. If you are attacked, you can use this to put off your attacker. Secondly, don't take anything with you that cannot easily be replaced like a passport or things of sentimental value. Leave jewellery and other valuables in your room when you go out. Always make sure you take something which will identify you, perhaps your student card or your driving licence. Thirdly, when you are out late at night, come home in twos. It's much safer if you're with a friend than on your own. And obviously, don't have very much money on you. Finally, if you do know you'll be late back and can't use public transport, tell someone else when you expect to be home and if there's a problem, they can raise the alarm. So, that's about all from me and I wish you a pleasant and safe stay here. Thank you.

That is the end of Section 1. You will have half a minute to check your answers (pause for 30 seconds).

Now turn to Section 2.

Margin labels: Q 4, Q 5, Q 6, Q 7, Q 8, Q 9, Q 10, example, Q 1, Q 2, Q 3

Section 2

You will hear two students, Sarah and John discussing their choices of courses to study. First you have some time to look at questions 11 to 15 (pause for 30 seconds).

Now listen carefully to the discussion and answer questions 11 to 15.

Sarah: Hi, John.

John: Hello, Sarah. What are you doing in here? Haven't all your exams finished?

Sarah: Well, yes, they have, but I've got to make my decisions for next year. I still haven't chosen what courses I'm going to do.

John: That's why I'm here. Why don't we have a look through the brochure together?

Sarah: That's a good idea. I'm not sure about some of these courses on medieval history.

John: No. In fact, I'm not sure about the whole second year. I was talking to Peter Lily the other day – you know, he's just finished the second year – and he was saying that the work load is higher in the second year because you have to read all these medieval documents in Latin. I mean, the first year's been pretty hard but next year will be worse. There are more assignments in the second year - it goes up to six a year for each course, doesn't it?

Q 11

Q 12

Sarah: Yes. But we've got the experience of the first year to build on, so it must get easier. And there isn't so much secondary material in the second year. There aren't so many books about the medieval period.

John: Don't you believe it! I think this year's going to be hard work!

Q 13

Sarah: Well, perhaps I'd better give up my job then.

John: You're working as well?

Sarah: Yeah, I've been working in the same place for over a year now. Only part-time, you know. Just Saturday mornings in the market. I mean, it doesn't pay much, but it's interesting and it gives me a bit of extra cash for my text books. Anyway, what about these courses? How many do we have to take? I remember Professor Bolt saying something about four courses in the second year, is that right? Or do we have to do a certain number of credits?

Q 14

Q 15

John: Both. We have to select four courses, but for some courses there are two parts. They count as one course. It's six in total, because everyone has to do Europe 1100-1500 and Chronicles of the Church. Anyway, when you've chosen your four courses, they should add up to 80 credits. Have you got the course brochure there?

Sarah: Yes. Look ... under ... second year history ... There it is.

You now have some time to read questions 16 to 20 (pause for 20 seconds).

Now listen to the rest of the discussion and answer questions 16 to 20.

John: Right. Yes, look. Most of these courses are 20 credits each, except for the two short courses about the Crusades. They're 10 each. Now, Medieval Society ... Hmm. What do you think?

Q 16

Sarah: Well, actually, I think it looks really good. Dr Smith is OK, and you don't have to buy any books except a study pack. The best thing is, there are no special requirements - no Latin or medieval English!

Q 17

John: The next one is Development of Technology with Mr Mills. Ah ... this is a good one. Peter recommended it. It's all about the way printing developed, and early science. In fact, I think I could get a copy of Bouchier's 'History of Science' from him. That means I wouldn't have to buy it.

Q 18

Sarah: That *does* look interesting. And that doesn't have any special requirements either. What's next...? Ah, here they are. 10 credits each, the Crusades. You need French to do them. I suppose a lot of the documents are in French.

John: That's strange, look. There are different teachers for each part. I expect that's why it's two modules. Dr Clare does the first part, but it's Dr Shaker and Professor Lord for the second one.

Q 19

Sarah: So that only leaves Peasants and Kings, with Dr Reeves. ... Oh, look, you have to know French for this one.

Q 20

John: Well, I must say I don't fancy any course that asks you to have Latin, but I think my French is good enough to read original sources.

Sarah: Yes, mine too. Well, what shall we choose ...?

That is the end of Section 2. You will have half a minute to check your answers (pause for 30 seconds).

Now turn to Section 3.

Section 3

You will hear an interview between Dr Mullet, a university lecturer and a student, Fayed. First you have some time to look at questions 21 to 25 (pause for 30 seconds).

Now listen carefully to the interview and answer questions 21 to 25.

Dr Mullet: So, Fayed, you found my office quite easily.

Fayed: Yes, thank you.

Dr Mullet: Thank you for coming such a long way for the interview. I believe you are from the Middle East. Now, Fayed, I really wanted to speak to you during this interview about two things - your exam results and your final-year dissertation. Your thesis, your dissertation, that was something quite special. Your personal tutor actually sent me a copy, and I must say that for a third year undergraduate <u>it's a very polished piece of work.</u>

Fayed: Thank you.

Q 21 Dr Mullet: <u>Yes, it's very promising.</u> Now, the thing is, your tutor tells me that you weren't all that happy with your exams ...

Fayed: Well ... The results aren't out yet, as you know. The first four were fine, but in the last three I lost my nerve a bit and didn't do so well. I know I didn't do as well as I

Q 22 could. <u>I was worried</u> when I'd handed in my exams.

Dr Mullet: Right. Well, exams are a bit of a game anyway. We can't all do well on the day. But here exam results are not everything, as you know - <u>I set great store by other factors in deciding whether we offer you a place on the Master's course.</u> Perhaps

Q 23 you could tell me a little about how you became interested in economics.

Fayed: Yes, of course. Well, I've always been interested in social and economic history, so from a very young age I read about the booms and crashes of the 19th and 20th centuries. I originally applied <u>to

Q 24 study history at university</u>, but when I got there I realised I had the chance to study economics at a high level, so I changed. My mother used to be an economist at the World Bank, so I had her to help me and guide me. Although she didn't help me write my final-year paper!

Dr Mullet: No, quite. Now, you're applying for the Master's course in the <u>Economics of the Q 25 Developing World</u>, taught by myself and Dr Branigan. Why this particular course?

Fayed: Well, I've read some of your work on the development of rural banks and I thought this was a good place to be. I mean, this is my first choice.

Now you have some time to read questions 26 to 30 (pause for 20 seconds).

Now listen to the rest of the interview and answer questions 26 to 30.

Dr Mullet: <u>And you're not worried about feeling homesick? You are still young, and Q 26 Australia is a very long way from your home.</u> I mean, your English is fine, there are no problems with language or attitude, but the distance from your family may make it hard for you at first.

Fayed: I've thought about that. But it's a problem wherever I go. <u>If I don't get in here, I'll probably take a place at a Q 27 university in England.</u> That's just as far from home!

Dr Mullet: I see, I see. And what are your long-term ambitions, Fayed? What do you want to do ultimately with your qualifications and your life?

Fayed: <u>I want to work in my country.</u> You know Q 28 there are some problems there, and I want to try to right some of them in the economic infrastructure.

Dr Mullet: I see. And this is your last interview, I believe. That gives you four weeks before the next term starts. What will you do during your holidays?

Fayed: Oh, I'm going to relax. I was going to work on my English, but in fact <u>I've got a couple of friends in Hamburg, so I think Q 29 I'll go and stay with them</u> instead as I've never been to Germany.

H: I see. Well, Fayed, as you know I can't give you a decision right away. However, I can tell you that you've made quite an impression with your application, and I think you should not worry too much about the place. <u>My decision will be made tomorrow</u> after I've seen the last Q 30 candidate, and I'll let you know within the next two weeks.

Fayed: Thank you very much.

Dr Mullet: Well, thank you for attending the interview.

That is the end of Section 3. You now have half a minute to check your answers (pause for 30 seconds).

Now turn to Section 4.

Section 4

You will hear a lecturer give a talk on nutrition. First you have some time to look at questions 31 to 40 (pause for 40 seconds).

Now listen carefully to the talk and answer questions 31 to 40.

Now, the topic of today's talk is nutrition - specifically, vitamins and minerals. I'll be dealing first with some of the most common misconceptions about them. Then I'm going to talk about what vitamins there are, where they come from, and the quantities we need. We'll have some time at the end of the talk for any questions you may have.

OK. Well, vitamins are known to the general public - in fact, the public knows more about them than it does about certain other key aspects of nutrition. **Q 31** One reason for this is that vitamins have been in the public eye for quite a while - at least since the middle of the 20th century, when their importance first became widely recognised. This awareness does mean that the public knows how important vitamins are - even if it doesn't mean that we all eat a healthy diet all the time. **Q 32** However, a problem does arise that is associated with this, which is the number of old wives' tales about vitamins. Usually these fallacies are not dangerous, but they do lead to an unnecessarily high intake of vitamin supplements. For example, it is widely held that high doses of vitamin C will cure colds and flu. **Q 33** I'd like to hit this one on the head - there is no evidence that any vitamin can cure anything! No, I'm afraid you'll just have to let time sort out your cold. And of course, the body can't store vitamin C, so those tablets you take are just an expensive waste of time.

Another common belief with no evidence is the idea that vitamin A helps you see in the dark. **Q 34** Actually, there is some truth in this one, because vitamin A is necessary for good vision. But in the dark, in real darkness, nobody can see. And of course, taking too much vitamin A can actually be bad for you. But perhaps the most misleading idea, heavily promoted by certain companies, is that vitamins will make you intelligent. **Q 35** Now, while a healthy diet is essential if you are to make the most of your intelligence, there is no evidence whatsoever that vitamin supplements can make the slightest bit of difference. *(Pause for 3 seconds).*

So what can vitamins do? Or, perhaps more accurately, why do we need them? Well, the answer is that we need them for all sorts of reasons.

Vitamin A, for example, also called retinol, is essential for good eyesight, especially at night, and to help us fight off infection and illness. We get it from **Q 36** liver, butter, egg yolks and milk.

Vitamin D, as is well known, is used to build strong **Q 37** teeth and bones, but it also helps us absorb calcium. Vitamin D is mainly formed in the skin through the action of sunlight. How much you need depends on different factors such as age and health.

Vitamin E, tocopherol, is less well-known, but is necessary in maintaining a healthy balance of fats in the body. We need 10-12 mg every day, and although **Q 38** some people take supplements, you can normally get what you need from a balanced diet.

The B complex includes vitamins B1, thiamine, B2, riboflavine, B6, pyridoxine and B12, cyanocobalamin. It performs many functions, including allowing our bodies to metabolise carbohydrates, forming healthy tissue, and perhaps most importantly, forming red **Q 39** blood cells to prevent pernicious anaemia. We need varying amounts of the B complex, and while most of us can get enough from a well-balanced diet, vegetarians may find themselves deficient in B12, which is only found in any noticeable quantity in meat, especially liver.

Finally, vitamin C is the one everyone knows. Ascorbic acid, as it's also known, helps fight infection, which perhaps accounts for the myth about preventing colds. It also helps protect against scurvy. We need 30 mg a day, and can only really get this amount from eating plenty of citrus fruit and fresh **Q 40** vegetables. Now, in a moment I'll be moving on to talk about how we can plan a diet which will supply all our vitamin needs. But before that, I'd like to look at some of the recent advances in our knowledge of the ways vitamin deficiencies can affect us ...
(fade)

That is the end of Section 4. You will have half a minute to check your answers. (pause for 30 seconds)

That is the end of the Listening Test.

You now have 10 minutes to transfer your answers to the Listening answer sheet. (pause for 10 minutes)

Please stop writing.

Listening Test 2

*You will hear a number of different recordings and you have to answer questions on what you hear. There will be time for you to read the instructions and you will have a chance to check your answers. The recordings will be heard only **once**. The test is in four sections. Record all your answers in your test book and at the end of the test you will be given 10 minutes to transfer your answers to a special answer sheet.*

Now turn to Section 1.

Section 1

You will hear a guide introducing tourists to the Red River Festival. First you will have some time to look at questions 1 to 4. (pause for 30 seconds)

You will see that there has been an example written for you. On this occasion only the conversation relating to the example will be played first. (listen to example being played)

*The festival is about arts and music so answer **c** has been circled.*

Now we will begin. You should answer the questions as you listen, as you will not hear the recording a second time. Listen to the talk carefully and answer questions 1 to 4.

example Now, as I'm sure you know, the Red River Festival - that is, the Red River International <u>Music</u> and <u>Arts Festival</u>, to give it its full name - is on while you are here, and I'm sure I speak for all the inhabitants of Red River in inviting you most cordially to attend. The festival takes place over a long weekend - that is,

Q 1 it starts on <u>the Friday afternoon and runs until Sunday evening</u>. Normally the festival would take place on 4th July, the same day as American Independence Day, but this year we have

Q 2 rescheduled <u>it for the fourth of August.</u>

Now, you can buy tickets for this festival either by the day or for the whole festival. The second option is cheaper, although of course not everyone can attend for the whole time. A day's ticket is $10, and it's $25 for the whole festival. That's very good value. If you want tickets, you are advised to get them early, because there are always more visitors than tickets. Space is limited, so buy early! You can get them direct from the festival organisers' headquarters, <u>the</u>

Q 3 <u>festival office</u>, and I'll give you that address later, or

Q 4 you can get them from any <u>of our three post offices</u> or one of the many bookshops in the town. Last year we issued them from tourist advice centres and the

Town Hall, but this year it was decided to limit the number of outlets to cut down on administrative costs.

Before the talk continues you have some time to read questions 5 to 10. (pause for 20 seconds) Now listen carefully and answer questions 5 to 10.

The weather is looking good. The forecasters expect it to be one of the <u>hottest and sunniest weekends</u> of   Q 5 the year, so it's perfect for the festival, although I would remind you to cover up and be aware of the dangers of too much sunshine. If it gets too hot for you, you could always stay inside for some of the indoor events. And of course you'll be able to get food - from sandwiches and snacks to barbecues, as well as ethnic fast food – <u>from several stands</u>. There   Q 6 will be a bar this year, but after last year we will only be selling soft drinks, <u>beer and wine</u>. We have   Q 7 decided not to bother with a spirits licence, there won't be any whisky on sale.

So, what's on? Well, I can only give you a flavour of the many attractions we have coming this year, but if I can name one of my personal favourites, you must see Petie's Dozen, a traditional <u>New Orleans</u> jazz   Q 8 band. They were here last year, and were so popular that we've invited them back. If you like <u>classical</u>   Q 9 <u>music</u>, we've got a string quartet from Poland, appropriately called Strings, playing classical favourites. We've also got rock bands, a blues band from the UK, a group of traditional Bavarian beer hall singers, and another of my favourites, The Fiddlers, who come from <u>Ireland</u>. Their special brand   Q 10 of folk music is popular all over the world. Moving on, then, to other attractions in the Red River area. For children, there's lots to do and see, from museums to theme parks ... (fade)

That is the end of Section 1. You will have half a minute to check your answers. (pause for 30 seconds)

Now turn to Section 2.

Section 2

You will hear a man and a female bank employee talking about getting a loan. First you have some time to look at questions 11 to 16. (pause for 30 seconds)

Now listen carefully to the discussion and answer questions 11 to 16.

(phone rings)

Woman: Good afternoon, County and District Bank Customer Services. Can I help you?

Man: Hello? I need to speak to someone about getting a loan, an overdraft.

Woman: Yes, perhaps I can help you. Do you bank with us, sir?

Man: Yes. My name is Mick O'Drew.

Woman: Sorry, sir. Your surname is ...

Q 11 Man: O'Drew. Mick O'Drew but my full name is Michael.

Woman: And can I have your account number, please, Mr O'Drew?

Man: Yes, it's 3926...1916.

Woman: That's ... fine. Now, I just need to confirm some details for security reasons. What is your address?

Q 12 Man: It's 24, Kilverton Drive. That's in Chalvey. That's C-H-A-L-V-E-Y. Er ... the postcode is ... SA3 9ER.

Woman: And your telephone number?

Man: 0458 ... 88320.

Woman: And can you tell me your date of birth, Mr O'Drew?

Q 13 Man: Yes. It's 23rd February 1967.

Woman: Thank you. Now, there are some gaps in your file here. I don't seem to have an address for you at work.

Man: No, when I joined your bank I didn't have a job.

Woman: Ah ...

Man: But I do now. I work for Culver Engineering. That's in Carbury. The address is 30, Works Yard, Carbury.

Woman: Could you repeat that?

Q 14 Man: Works Yard. W-O-R-K-S Y-A-R-D. It's two words.

Woman: Right. Thank you. Do you have a work telephone number where we can contact you, please?

Q 15 Man: Yes, it's ...0912...795...09.

Woman: 7509.

Man: No, it's 79509.

Woman: Oh, right. Thank you. How long have you been there, Mr O'Drew?

Man: Um... I started in 1997...no, 1998.

Woman: OK, that's fine. And can you tell me your current salary, please?

Q 16 Man: Well, I'm not sure exactly, but it's about, er ... 18,000 pounds.

You now have some time to look at questions 17 to 20 (pause for 20 seconds).

Now listen to the rest of the discussion and answer questions 17 to 20.

Woman: Now, you would like an overdraft. Do you have any other major debts?

Man: What do you mean?

Woman: Well, are you paying a mortgage on your house?

Man: Yes...

Woman: How much is that every month?

Q 17 Man: It's about 450 pounds.

Woman: I see... And do you have any credit cards or storecards?

Q 18 Man: Yes, I pay 45 pounds a month in credit card charges. Oh, and about 19 pounds a month for my storecard - that's with J.H. Olney, the clothes shop.

Woman: Do you have any personal loans, or hire purchase agreements?

Q 19 Man: None whatsoever.

Q 20 Woman: Right, well, the loan shouldn't be a problem. I can set it up for you in the morning. I've set your limit at 250 pounds, although you can raise this to £300 if you're still having problems. Just give us a ring if you need to.

Man: Oh, that's great. Thank you. Goodbye.

Woman: Goodbye, sir.

That is the end of Section 2. You will have half a minute to check your answers (pause for 30 seconds).

Now turn to Section 3.

Section 3

You will hear a conversation between two students, David and Maria, about the candidates for an election for student officers. First you have some time to look at questions 21 to 23 (pause for 20 seconds).

Now listen carefully to the conversation and answer questions 21 to 23.

David: Hi Maria. Have you voted yet?

Maria: Oh, hello, David. Erm, what did you say?

David: Have you voted yet? You know, in the student union elections?

Maria: Well, no... I mean, they've only just released the names of the final candidates. The first round elections were only held last week.

David: But I've voted already!

Maria: Yes... but that's the first round. You know how this works, don't you?

David: Well, not exactly. I mean, I thought you just voted...

Q 21 Maria: It's pretty simple, but it's made more complicated because this university has four colleges, not just one. Each college can have many candidates for each post. These are reduced to a logical number, then the real voting takes place.

David: So what did I vote for last week?

Maria: That was the first round, like I said. You voted for the candidates for Peterborough College, that's all. There are also candidates from the other three colleges.

David: Oh, I see.

Maria: **Q 22** Well, there are seven positions to apply for in the union, although two of those are dealt with later in the year. That's the president and the vice-president. Anyway, each college sends one candidate on to the second round, so that's four in all for each post - in other words ...

David: In other words, it's 20 candidates. That's quite a lot!

Maria: It isn't when you think that there are 14,000 students at this college!

David: No, I suppose not. Can they all vote?

Maria: Yes. Part-time and full-time students - everyone. But most don't. **Q 23** Only about a quarter of those eligible to actually bothered.

You now have some time to look at questions 24 to 30 (pause for 20 seconds).

Now listen to the rest of the conversation and answer questions 24 to 30.

David: So who are the candidates from our college?

Maria: There was a leaflet about it this week. Some of the students stood as candidates for several posts before the final ones were selected. I think Jenny de Groot is standing **Q 24** for Women's Officer. She wanted to be **Q 25** Finance Officer but Law got that post.

David: She seems to be more suited to working for the female students here.

Maria: **Q 26** Yes, I like her – she's the best person for the job. I'm not sure I'd support Michael McCarthy for his post. He's putting up for Entertainments Officer.

David: Doesn't he arrange the Saturday night band for the college? And the sports events? Surely he'd be ideal — he has so much experience.

Maria: Maybe. I don't think he chooses the right kind of groups for the college — he's too **Q 27** wayout. He's not my choice.

David: Who's the candidate to be Overseas Officer?

Maria: A Chinese student who's been here for just over a year. She's the president of the Chinese club and she organises some interesting cultural evenings for them. She seems to be quite capable.

David: Do you really think so? She's in my seminar group for linguistics. Her English is quite poor and she's so shy she never mixes with us.

Maria: Oh, there are 30 different nationalities here, so she'd need to be more sociable. Perhaps Vikram Patel would have been a **Q 28** better choice.

David: Yes, I think so. Who did you say was finance officer? Law? Charles Law? he does accountancy so he should be able to cope with the post. He'd be responsible for a lot of money.

Maria: I've always thought he was unreliable and didn't he fail some of his exams in the first year? Doesn't sound too competant to me. **Q 29**

David: OK. yes. You're probably right! Who's the other person on the list?

Maria: It's Brian McKay.

David: Oh, McKay. He's quite a character. What position is he standing for?

Maria: He wants to be the Liaison Officer. The person who lets the teaching staff know about any problems the students might have. He's such a sociable person he'd be a great communicator.

David: Yes, he's articulate and well-organised but **Q 30** he wouldn't be my first choice. Anyway they're only the candidates from Peterborough College so we'll have to wait for the results of the real election next week to see who actually gets each post.

Maria: Yes, we can discuss this again.

That is the end of Section 3. You now have half a minute to check your answers (pause for 30 seconds).

Now turn to Section 4.

Section 4

You will hear a lecturer giving a talk on languages. First you have some time to look at questions 31 to 40 (pause for 40 seconds).

Now listen carefully to the talk and answer questions 31 to 40.

[Lecturer]
Thank you all for coming. Are we all here ...? Right, well, let's begin ...
This lecture, as you know, is the third in our course, Introduction to Linguistics. Today we'll be looking at

Q 31 a variety of different languages, not any one specific one, and we'll be looking especially at languages which can help us understand how both language and languages evolve. Another issue that we will be exploring is the way in which languages have changed
Q 32 over time. These are fairly complex areas, and they have proved to be rather difficult to grasp. There are many different theories, some of which we'll look at today. (pause for 3 seconds)

[Lecturer]

But first I want to talk briefly about a few different ways of looking at a language. Now, the language we all speak - English - is what is called a "natural"
Q 33 language, like French, German, Greek. What do we mean by that? Well, it's a difficult term to define, because most languages have evolved naturally, except for a very few such as Esperanto, which was invented in the 19th century. So I suppose that what we mean by "natural" is a language which we consider stable, fixed, not constantly changing. Now, as we know, all
Q 34 languages are in fact constantly changing, so it's something of a misnomer, but let's put it another way: "natural" languages are considered by us to be permanent: they didn't appear suddenly, they grew up out of other things.

Now, I want to contrast these languages with two other kinds of language, *pidgin* languages and *creole* languages. A pidgin language is a language which is forced into being by circumstances - usually some sort of situation where two groups meet and don't speak
Q 35 each other's language, and they invent an intermediary language, usually for the purpose of trade, or sometimes war. An example is Tok Pisin, which is a pidgin spoken in Papua New Guinea.

A creole language, on the other hand, develops
Q 36 from a pidgin into a full language. This happens when the pidgin starts having native speakers – that is, people whose first language is the pidgin. This happened in the case of the French creole spoken in
Q 37 New Orleans, for example.

Pidgins are found all over the world, especially in areas which are or were once important trade routes.
Q 38 The Caribbean, China, India, the Pacific ... Basically, pidgins can be identified with one or two important characteristics. They are made up of parts of the two languages spoken by the group that have met - the trading groups or whatever - and they are usually based on a simplified form of one of those languages. That is, their grammar is a less complicated version of the grammar in one language. They use vocabulary from both languages, but there are fewer words, so
Q 39 each word often has more than one meaning. For example, in Tok Pisin, "gras-bilong-face" means "hair" or "beard". The pronunciation is also made simpler, as

pidgins lose the complex vowels of the parent languages.

Creoles, on the other hand, formed when pidgins are learnt as a first language, are just as complex as so-called natural languages. They are expanded pidgins. There is often a considerable element of politicalisation, as the emphasis moves from *communication*, which to pidgin speakers is most important, to *community*, which is the mark of a creole. That is, a creole is a community who speak a different, marginalised language. They often have to struggle to get their language recognised. Q 40

As to where pidgins come from, there are basically two theories. The first claims that all pidgins are descended from a medieval trading language, what you might call the first pidgin, called Sabir. This is believed to have been based on Portuguese. It was spread as the Portuguese traders went from place to place. (fade)

That is the end of Section 4. You will have half a minute to check your answers. (pause for 30 seconds)

That is the end of the Listening Test.

You now have 10 minutes to transfer your answers to the Listening answer sheet. (pause for 10 minutes)

Please stop writing.

Listening Test 3

*You will hear a number of different recordings and you have to answer questions on what you hear. There will be time for you to read the instructions and you will have a chance to check your answers. The recordings will be heard only **once**. The test is in four sections. Record all your answers in your test book and at the end of the test you will be given 10 minutes to transfer your answers to a special answer sheet.*

Now turn to Section 1.

Section 1

You will hear a Student Union representative talking to some new students. First you will have some time to look at questions 1 to 7 (pause for 30 seconds).

You will see that there has been an example written for you. On this occasion only the conversation relating to the example will be played first (listen to example being played).

The questionnaire is about food on the campus so the word food has been written in the gap.

Now we will begin. You should answer the questions as you listen as you will not hear the recording a second time.

Listen to the talk carefully and answer questions 1 to 7.

[murmur of speaking]

A. Hullo, everyone, and welcome to Borchester University. If you'd like to split into small groups of about ten, a guide will take you around the campus - the first thing they'll show you is the most important - where to get <u>food</u>! OK, please divide into smaller groups now, the guides are here on the left.

example

[Guide] Right, ... nine, ten - that's about right. OK let's start. As the co-ordinator said, we'll look at where to eat on campus first. The principal place to buy food is here - the Main Refectory. As you can see this is large - it holds about five hundred people - so it's very busy.

What can you buy here? They always have a good choice. Usual choices are vegetarian, fish, <u>pasta and salad</u> - as well as a main choice menu, including the budget choice. Sometimes they do special menus for a week - last week it was Chinese food. Mmm - I remember they had some wonderful choices.

Q 1

[laughter]

Of course, to get the best choice you need to get here early. The main hall is open from <u>11:30 to half past two</u> - but by about two the choices are rather reduced. Unless you like chips and pies, that is - the budget menu is always available!

Q 2

What's the cost here? Well, it varies - from <u>about £1.50 for the budget meal to £3</u>. It sounds expensive, but if you eat here you probably won't want to eat so much in the evening as the portions are huge.

Q 3

OK, so much for the refectory. The next place to eat is the café near the Arts Building - that's here on the map. This is small - much smaller, <u>with only space for about 50 people</u>. It's also a shop, so it's very busy all day. It's open from nine in the morning until six in the evening. What can you buy here? Well, really only tea, coffee, hot chocolate and sandwiches. <u>The cost of a meal is about £1.15</u>. One nice thing about here is that you can surf the Internet while you eat - absolutely free, as long as you are a customer, of course. There are six computers for customers to use. Oh, I said there's a shop too - it sells all the usual things, chocolate, newspapers, sweets, cakes and bottled drinks. It's very convenient.

Q 4

Q 5

Another nice place to eat is the <u>bar area in the theatre</u> - again this is small, but there's more space than the café and no shop, so it tends to be less crowded. It is still quite busy though, because it's very comfortable with nice chairs. It's open from 10 to 4. What can you get to eat here? Again, it's really only drinks like tea and coffee and <u>toasted sandwiches</u>. The toasted sandwiches here are better since they also have a garnish - tomatoes and lettuce - with them, but the average meal costs more - about £1.30. One problem is that they run out quickly here - you are not likely to find much to eat after about 1.30.

Q 6

Q 7

Before the talk continues you have some time to read questions 8 to 10. (pause for 20 seconds). Now listen carefully and answer questions 8 to 10.

Well, that's the general information about where you can eat on campus. But you know, those places are not just for eating and drinking. The Main Refectory has a string quartet of music students playing every <u>Thursday</u> at lunchtime and on Tuesdays and Fridays the Theatre Bar offers lunchtime <u>jazz concerts at one o' clock</u>. They 're always popular and the bar fills up by noon, so make sure you get there early.

Q 8

Q 9

Now, I can see some of you are smoking. This is only allowed in certain areas of the campus and never in the library or eating places. Oh no, sorry, it *is* allowed in <u>the Main Refectory</u> but only in a small section in the corner. There were suggestions that the Theatre Bar would be a smoking area but this created quite a debate among students so a final decision hasn't as yet been made.

Q 10

Thanks for your attention. Now your guide will take you on your tour.

That is the end of Section 1. You will have half a minute to check your answers (pause for 30 seconds).

Now turn to Section 2.

Section 2

You will hear two students, Amanda and Barry discussing the disposal of their household rubbish.

First you have some time to look at questions 11 to 15 (pause for 20 seconds).

Now listen carefully to the discussion and answer questions 11 to 15.

Amanda: We really had better sort this waste out - there's quite a lot of it now.

Barry: Yes, it's probably worthwhile taking this lot to the recycling centre now - there's at least a full car-load.

Amanda: Yes, but first we need to sort it all out - we won't be able to do that once we arrive there.

Barry: OK, so what do we do?

Amanda: That's easy – we put each type into labelled boxes.

Barry: You mean sort them out into different materials?

Amanda: Yes, that's right.

Barry: OK, it seems quite straightforward. What shall we start with? What about the glass?

Amanda: Good idea – first let's put all these bottles in.

Q 11 Barry: Yes, but we shouldn't put that milk bottle in - that should go back to the <u>milkman</u>.

Amanda: Yes, you are right – this is a returnable bottle too - it goes back to the local shop.

Q 12 Barry: <u>This broken mirror</u> can go with the glass, can't it?

Amanda: Yes, of course, but be careful of your fingers.

Barry: OK, what's next.

Amanda: Paper, I think. We should tie up all those piles of old newspapers and magazines.

Barry: What about these <u>yellow telephone books</u>?

Amanda: I think I remember reading that we shouldn't put those in when I last went there - we had better not. We 'll put them **Q 13** in the <u>general rubbish</u>.

Barry: And these paperback books?

Amanda: No, definitely not those - they should be **Q 14** put into <u>the charity container</u>. They can re-sell those for charity.

Barry: There are some old car-batteries here – they look heavy. Let's lift them out here.

Amanda: Be careful! Lift them carefully, don't hurt your back - bend your knees not your back. And be careful you don't spill any acid – it will burn you!

Barry: It's a pity Britain doesn't have any system to collect these yet. They will just be dumped, together with all the <u>general</u> **Q 15** <u>rubbish</u>.

Amanda: That's terrible! Doesn't anyone do something with them?

Barry: Well, if we lived in Germany, Denmark or Sweden we could recycle them, but not in the UK – at least, not yet.

Amanda: There are bundles of old magazines and newspapers here too. I think we put these in the general rubbish.

Q 16 Barry: No, there's a special <u>container for paper</u>.

It's all recycled and they make other products like writing and kitchen paper with it.

Amanda: Actually, I think you'll find they can't do that with <u>magazines</u> as it's a different **Q 17** quality paper. They *do* go with the rest of the household refuse. Oh, look, plastic bottles – lots of them ...

You now have some time to read questions 18 to 20 (pause for 20 seconds). Now listen to the rest of the discussion and answer questions 18 to 20.

Amanda: Oh look, plastic bottles – lots of them!

Barry: Well, you know how much cola they had at the party, that's where most of it's from.

Amanda: Well, all the soft-drink bottles can be put together, what about the other plastics here?

Barry: Some things have <u>a code</u> – yes, look here, **Q 18** these two are the same. We just need to look for the code on the plastic. That will tell us where we have to put the bottles.

Amanda: Any bottle without a code – well, we'll just have to check when we get there.

Barry: There won't be too many – anyway, they do have a technician to <u>offer advice</u> when **Q 19** you get to the re-cycling centre.

Amanda: OK – we've nearly finished. What about this bag of old clothes?

Barry: That's easy! The charities take those as they are. and they sort them out. Then they can sell the clothes which are still in a good condition and they can make a lot of money out of them. The bad ones can be sold as rags – the <u>paper industry</u> takes **Q 20** those.

Amanda: It's amazing what can be done with things we throw away.

Barry: If we don't try to recycle then the future of the planet. (fade)

That is the end of Section 2. You will have half a minute to check your answers (pause for 30 seconds).

Now turn to Section 3.

106

Section 3

You will hear a talk given by Mrs. Beverley Evans about the Borchester Hospital Trust. First you have some time to look at questions 21 to 24 (pause for 30 seconds).

Now listen carefully to the talk and answer questions 21 to 24.

Dr Groves:
Welcome, everyone, to this final session of the Borchester Health Authority's Nurses Orientation Programme. We're very pleased to welcome Mrs Beverly Evans, who is the chairman, or should I say chairperson, of the Borchester Hospital Trust. All you nurses will know how valuable the work of the trust is to us. And Beverly is going to bring us up to date with some of the things the trust has been doing. Beverly ...

(smattering of applause)

Mrs Beverly Evans:
Thank you, Dr, Groves, for inviting me to talk to this group. I am happy to report to you on our progress over the last few months.

Well, I am sure you'd like me to start with the good news. Most importantly, I can report on the Hospital Trust's standards for last year. Well, one rough guide is how happy the public were with our service. I am happy to report that 5961 letters of appreciation were received by the Trust, whilst there were only 57 letters of complaint. I am sure that we don't want any letters of complaint at all, but I am sure you'll feel that this is a good result.

Q 21

(murmurs of appreciation, subdued clapping)

On the topic of public relations, we have recently established a "Visitors Charter" to inform the public what standards to expect. These standards are now displayed in all patient areas, for instance on ward notice boards.

Q 22

An area of particular concern is that of patients with special needs. One recent initiative is a policy where all patients who have hearing problems have their records marked with a "sympathetic ear" symbol - only with their consent, of course. This will mean that anyone dealing with those whose hearing is impaired will be aware of the problem from the onset.

Q 23

Now, on to general topics. The main entrance is being improved. You've all seen the plans, I am sure, and you've walked round the building work. Sorry about that. Well, the work actually started a few months ago. I am very happy to tell you the work is progressing well, and is on-budget and on time. By next June, we will have a brand new entrance hall, which will be much better than the old one.

Q 24

You now have some time to read questions 25 to 30 (pause for 20 seconds). Now listen to the rest of the talk and answer questions 25 to 30.

We've received a few suggestions which would help patients. One interesting one is that staff who can speak another language should wear a badge to show this. Well, we've worked on this, and have now identified speakers of Welsh, Urdu, and Arabic. Soon these staff will be sent badges to wear to show they are bilingual. We are hoping to add further languages to this scheme very soon - by the autumn at least.

Q 25
Q 26
Q 27

Now fundraising! As you know, our local newspaper is supporting the Cancer Appeal. The public's response continues to be excellent and many donations are received every day. Many members of the public have contacted us with fund-raising plans. There are a lot of interesting ideas, but one really good one is for an open-air twilight dinner in the local park - but, given our weather, I feel that a large tent would be a good precaution. Other more traditional ideas are for sponsored bike rides, and sponsored sea swimming. Details of these, and the necessary sponsor forms, will be available shortly.

Q 28

Q 29

Lastly a report on patient feedback within the Chemotherapy Unit. We undertook a survey 18 months ago, questioning 50 first attenders and 150 re-attenders in the unit. I am sure you'll be happy to hear that all, yes all, of these patients felt they were made welcome and were treated courteously at all times. Nearly all, 96%, felt they had their treatment explained satisfactorily, and 98% found the facilities in the Day Unit to be very good. A small number of areas need to be improved: one is more car parking, more toilet facilities and better areas for private discussions. But I am happy that the survey was so positive...

Q 30

That is the end of section 3. You will have half a minute to check your answers (pause for 30 seconds).

Now turn to section 4.

Section 4

You will hear two friends, Ann and Geoff, discussing their completion of a student questionnaire.

First you have some time to look at questions 31 to 40 (pause for 40 seconds).

Now listen carefully to the talk and answer questions 31 to 40.

Prof Merrick

... so if you would all be kind enough to fill in these questionnaires before you go, I would be most grateful. I do take your comments very seriously, and if you don't tell me if something doesn't work, then I can't do anything about it, can I? Anyway, take a moment now ...

Ann: Geoff, you've got to help me with this. I never know what to write for these things.

Geoff: Well, the beginning is easy enough, Ann. You know what year we're in.

Ann: The first year, so that's level one? Okay, I'll underline that.

Geoff: And the title of the course is *An Introduction to the History of the South Pacific.*

Q 31 Ann: *An Introduction to South Pacific History, actually.*

Geoff: And the teacher is Professor Merrick.

Q 32 Ann: And Dr Smith. She was nice.

Geoff: I don't remember her. Was that one of the lectures I couldn't attend?

Ann: Actually, she did two sessions in January and you had the flu then. Do you remember?

Geoff: Oh yes.

Ann: But what's the type of teaching? We have lectures and seminars. Should I underline both? Or write something in Other?

Geoff: No, a seminar course is one where there are no lectures, just seminar meetings and discussions. The lecture course assumes there'll be some tutorials as well. But it is just

Q 33 considered a lecture course. Underline that.

Ann: Okay, now for the hard part. These statements about the course. It's 1 if we disagree and 4 if we agree. Right?

Geoff: Right. Well, the module has clearly stated aims and objectives. Surely you can give that a 4?

Ann: Yes, I agree.

Geoff: And for number 2, I thought the teaching methods were fine and encouraged me to

Q 34 participate. Give that a 4 too.

Ann: You hypocrite! You hardly ever got out of bed for the classes. They certainly didn't encourage you to participate. You should give it a 1 or 2.

Geoff: But that was my problem and not his. Professor Merrick is good and he encouraged me. I just didn't respond... He
deserves a 4.   Q 35

Ann: Okay, then. Number 3 the same. Number 4, an up-to-date reading list. Well, I think that's true. I'd give it a 4.

Geoff: I'm not so sure about that. Every time I went to the library I could only get old books if I could get anything at all. I say a 2 for that or even 1.

Ann: You're being unfair Geoff. You were unable to get the books because you left writing the essay until too late and other students had the books out. Let's compromise and give it
3. What about book provision in the library   Q 36
being adequate? It's number 5. I think I
would give that a couple of points because a   Q 37
lot of books on the reading list only have one copy and, with over 100 people on the course, that's not enough. But the reading list itself is good.

Geoff: Okay. But the time on each topic is fine.

Ann: Yes. That's a 4, I guess.

Geoff: For number 7, the feedback question, I think I'd give that a 4 too. He wrote some very helpful comments on my essays.

Ann: I thought I'd have liked the opportunity to talk through the ideas in the essay with Professor Merrick at more length. Just an hour or so. A 2, maybe?

Geoff: I think that would be hard. You said yourself that there are more than 100 students on the course. If he spent an hour with everyone, you work it out. That's ... two and a half weeks' work.

Ann: Well, a 3 then. Numbers 8 and 9 get 4s.   Q 38
Number 10, adequacy of classroom and facilities.

Geoff: Now that is a problem. The room's not big   Q 39
enough for so many people and the chairs don't have those things on the side so you can make notes – what are they called?

Ann: Wings. And it is ever so hot in that room with   Q 40
all those people there.

Geoff: As Professor Merrick says, if we don't complain about it, no-one will change the room. In fact, I think you should say exactly what the problems are in the Other Comments section. Leave out the hot bit - that's just a result of the fact that the room isn't designed for 100 or so people. We should write down our comments though.

Ann: Okay, I'll put our two complaints on paper.

That is the end of Section 4. You will have half a minute to check your answers. (pause for 30 seconds)

That is the end of the Listening Test.

You now have 10 minutes to transfer your answers to the Listening answer sheet. (pause for 10 minutes)

Please stop writing.

Listening Test 4

*You will hear a number of different recordings and you have to answer questions on what you hear. There will be time for you to read the instructions and you will have a chance to check your answers. The recordings will be heard only **once**. The test is in four sections. Record all your answers in your test book and at the end of the test you will be given 10 minutes to transfer your answers to a special answer sheet.*

Now turn to Section 1.

Section 1

You will hear a talk given by a guide to a group of tourists going on a coach tour of the capital cities of Europe. First you will have some time to look at questions 1 to 8 (pause for 30 seconds).

You will see that there has been an example written for you. On this occasion only the conversation relating to the example will be played first.

The tour leader's first name is Jenny so the word Jenny has been written in the gap.

Now we will begin. You should answer the questions as you listen as you will not hear the recording a second time.

Listen to the talk carefully and answer questions 1 to 8.

(fade in, person counting to themselves)
Forty-one, forty-two, forty-three. That's everyone.

(raised voice speaking to a whole bus)

Okay, if you can just bear with me for a moment or two. Hello everyone. Thanks for getting here on time. We'll get underway directly and make the first leg of our trip. But first let me introduce myself to you. I'm *example* Jenny Allen and I'm going to be your tour leader on this trip of European capitals. If you have any problems or difficulties, or if you want to know more about something, then ask me and I'll do my very best

to help you. And this is Ray, Ray Smith, who is our   Q 1
driver for this tour. And welcome especially to Chardra and Indira. They've just finished their university exams and are celebrating with a tour before going home to India.

Now, Eurobus's European Capitals Tour. Five capitals in six days. I gave you our itinerary as you   Q 2
were coming aboard so let me take you through it. It hasn't changed from the time you booked, I promise, but various things we couldn't put in the brochure have been confirmed now and I can tell you about them. This is day 1 and we're going to drive from here, down the M1 to London which will be the first of our capitals. We expect to arrive in London, at about 1.00 in the afternoon. There will be a break for coffee on the way, probably around 11am, at Northampton. After lunch at 3.00, there's a tour of   Q 3
the the sites of London: Buckingham Palace, the Houses of Parliament, Trafalgar Square and so on. At 5.00 we'll book you into your hotel for the night. We have arranged some tea but we need to leave at 6.30 promptly please, to get you into the show on   Q 4
time. As we hoped, we're all going to see Abba the Musical (muted cheers), so you can all sing along. We'll be back at the hotel by 11.00 and, if you want, you can have a drink or something else to eat then.   Q 5

Day 2. Breakfast is arranged for 7.00. We've booked a full breakfast and the bus will leave at 8.30. We must be on time for this because we've got to book into the Eurostar by 9.30 at the latest and we can never be sure of the traffic, so we need to give ourselves plenty of time. There're a buffet bar on board Eurostar all the way to Paris, so you can get   Q 6
coffee or snacks or anything during the time it takes to go to Paris, which is our second capital. We should arrive at ten to one. We'll go straight to the hotel. By the way, it will be the *King George* Hotel, not the   Q 7
Victor Hugo Hotel as originally listed. Don't worry, it is actually a much better hotel. The rest of the itinerary in Paris remains the same. Lunch followed by a tour of the city – the Eiffel Tower, the Arc de Triomphe, Notre Dame. You're free for 3 hours after   Q 8
5 to go wherever you want and we're booked at 8.30 for dinner at *L' Escargot*. It has four Michelin Stars and will be a meal, I promise you, you won't forget.

Before the talk continues you have some time to read qauestion 9 and 10 (pause for 20 seconds). Now listen carefully and answer questions 9 and 10.

Now I appreciate this is a lot to take in, so I won't go through the rest of it in any detail - although you can ask me later if you want. I'll just point to some of the minor changes so they don't surprise you later. Day three we'll drive to Brussels. The trip round the chocolate factory is now confirmed. It will be the Leonidas factory. I'm looking forward to that. There won't be a bus tour of Brussels because there are

Q 9 <u>elections</u> on day three and large parts of the city will be blocked off, so we've arranged a walking tour instead. If any of you feel that doesn't appeal, then see me and my colleagues in head office will try to arrange something else instead. Day four is Luxembourg and there's no change there. Day five is Berlin. Day six is Amsterdam, not exactly a capital city but the biggest Dutch town. We have been

Q 10 successful at getting you into the <u>Van Gogh</u> art exhibition there. I know some of you will enjoy that. Then it is back on the ferry and we hope to be in Wolverhampton by midnight.

That is the end of Section 1. You will have half a minute to check your answers (pause for 30 seconds).

Now turn to Section 2.

Section 2

You will hear two students, Debbie and Andrew, talking about a university assignment. First you have some time to look at questions 11 to 14 (pause for 30 seconds).

Now listen carefully to the discussion and answer questions 11 to 14.

Debbie: Hi Andrew. I told Dr Ball that you were under the weather and he gave me the details of the next assignment so you can get on with it when you're feeling better.

Andrew: Oh, thanks, Debbie. Another essay?

Debbie: Actually, it's not an essay. We've got to give a presentation to the rest of the group

Q 11 and prepare <u>handouts</u> for them.

Andrew: We? Is it group work?

Debbie: It's you, me, Jessica and Mark. It's a business planning exercise. We'll take a hypothetical new business and we'll prepare a business plan for it and then explain it to Dr Ball. We've got six weeks to do it.

Andrew: So how do we approach the task?

Debbie: Dr Ball suggested we took the idea of running a paramedical training company in the Middle East.

Andrew: Okay, so who's doing what?

Debbie: Well, we had a chat and we thought you could help Mark. There's quite a bit of medical training in the Middle East, so we Q 12 can get quite accurate financial <u>costing</u> into this. Mark will do that. He's good at figures.

Andrew: That's good. I can help. I had a job last summer in an accountant's office and I've got <u>experience</u> with figures. Anyway, Q 13 what are you and Jessica going to do?

Debbie: We can do some <u>more research on the smaller companies</u> in the area who do Q 14 medical training while you and Mark can concentrate on the bigger firms. Both Jessica and I have good research skills.

You now have some time to read questions 15 to 20 (pause for 20 seconds). Now listen to the rest of the discussion and answer questions 15 to 20.

Andrew: Seems you've been busy planning the whole project!

Debbie: Well, six weeks seems like a long time but we've got some mid-term tests in a <u>fortnight</u> Q 15 so I think we'd better get on with this presentation as soon as possible.

Andrew: You're right. What about arranging when we can meet to check on each other's progress.

Debbie: That's going to be a bit tricky. Jessica won't be here from next Monday to Saturday as she's got to <u>have some minor surgery</u>. Q 16

Andrew: Nothing to worry about, I hope.

Debbie: No, it's just something routine. But Mark will be away at the weekend and won't be back until Tuesday or even Wednesday. His brother's getting married and he's going to be best man.

Andrew: That means neither of them will have much time to be working on our project in the next couple of weeks then.

Debbie: No, and as we'll all have to be studying for our mid-term tests as well, <u>I think you and I will be bearing the brunt of the work in the initial stages</u>, Andrew. Q 17

Andrew: That's fair enough Debbie but I hope they'll pull their weight later. I don't want you and I to have to do all the work. We've got to pass these tests too!

Debbie: You're right but I don't think Jessica and Mark are the type of people to shirk their responsibilities. Anyway, when are we going to have this meeting?

Andrew: What about next Wednesday?

Debbie: Well, Jessica will be fine by then but Mark isn't sure if he'll be back or not so what about **Q 18** the following day to be certain?

Andrew: Agreed. But where? We all live in different parts of the town so how about the Student Union bar?

Debbie: Don't you think it would be rather noisy?

Andrew: Not if we meet in the morning. I haven't got any lectures until 2o'clock.

Debbie: None of us has. No, wait, Mark has one at 11 but maybe he could miss that this time and copy up the notes. Let's say we'll meet at the **Q 19** bar but a bit later, at noon.

Andrew: Good, that's sorted out. Now, who's actually going to give the presentation? Jessica has such a quiet voice and Mark's Scottish accent is difficult to understand.

Debbie: It's not that strong! Sometimes I can't work out what you are saying, Andrew!

Andrew: OK. I admit my accent is not that clear. But remember we have a couple of Japanese students in the group. It wouldn't be fair on them to have to listen to any of us.

Q 20 Debbie: We can decide that later. We don't have to worry about that yet. I'll have to rush. I've got a lecture in 10 minutes. So, get well soon.

Andrew: Thanks, Debbie. We'll be in touch. Bye.

That is the end of Section 2. You will have half a minute to check your answers (pause for 30 seconds).

Now turn to Section 3.

Section 3

You will hear a conversation between Mrs Davis and a lady she is interviewing called Gina. First you have some time to look at questions 21 to 27. (pause for 30 seconds)

Now listen carefully to the talk and answer questions 21 to 27.

Gina: Mrs Davis, Hello. Can I see you for a moment?

Q 21 Mrs Davis: Ah, Gina, hello.

Gina: Hello, Mrs Davis. It's about the job as assistant in the language department. I hope I'm not disturbing you.

Mrs Davis: No ... er, no, no. Of course not. I was rather thinking you were coming to see me with the others tomorrow. Didn't I make an appointment for you?

Gina: Yes, but I've got a bit of a problem. I have to go to London tomorrow to meet my **Q 22** father. He's coming over here for a business meeting. I wondered if we could rearrange it?

Mrs Davis: Yes of course. Right ... Now, I got your application form, haven't I? Yes, here we are, Gina Barraco. So, tomorrow's out. How about Thursday afternoon at 2:00 **Q 23** o'clock?

Gina: That would be fine.

Mrs Davis: That's perfect. Actually, I'm glad you came in because there were one or two things our Personnel Department wasn't sure about when they checked your **Q 24** application and I can ask you about them now. How do you think you'd manage – I mean, your spoken English is pretty good – how do you think you'd manage the administrative side of things in English? I need to comment on the level of your English.

Gina: Well, actually, I'm not too worried about that kind of thing. Before I came here I worked as a clerk in a bank for two **Q 25** summers. I'm not a qualified secretary or anything, but I'm fairly organised and I'm good at getting things done. I'm not so sure exactly how good my English is, but then I'll be teaching in Italian, won't I?

Mrs Davis: Yes... I think your English will be fine and the department would always welcome a good administrator. Now, tell me about your academic commitments next year. You've applied for a place on the Master's scheme, haven't you? How **Q 26** would you fit that in with your work for us?

Gina: Well, it's part-time over two years, so apart from the reading, which I can do at the weekend and in the evenings, it's about four class hours a week. Anyway, I don't know if I'll be accepted on it, although I feel quite excited. I had the interview last Monday with Dr Marplot, and it went really well. He asked me exactly the questions I wanted.

Mrs Davis: That's good. Now, the post we're looking to fill is to teach Italian media – in Italian, **Q 27** of course. That involves reading and discussion classes mainly, although you'd be expected to help the undergraduates with their language as well. You can speak to the other assistants about how it works, exactly - there is one in each language department. They're mainly Europeans, although I think we've got one Russian, too.

You now have some time to read questions 28 to 30 (pause for 20 seconds). Now listen to the rest of the discussion and answer questions 28 to 30.

Gina: Can I ask something?

Mrs Davis: Of course.

Q 28

Gina: Well, I think one of the biggest problems for me is going to be <u>money</u>. I get a tiny grant, as you know, and my parents are not rich, so I need to know how much I'd be paid.

Mrs Davis: Of course. Well, the pay is not great - it works out at 150 pounds a week. But the good thing is, you wouldn't have to pay tax. Oh, and you'd be able to keep your

Q 29

<u>college accommodation</u> if you wanted to. That would be cheaper than living out.

Gina: Yes. Oh, that sounds fine.

Mrs Davis: Well, as you know, I've got to see the other two applicants tomorrow. Then it'll take a week or so to discuss everything with Dr Santini, the head of Italian ... I

Q 30

expect we'll know in <u>a couple of weeks</u>. OK? We'll let you all know then.

Gina: Thank you very much, Mrs Davis.

Mrs Davis: Not at all, Gina. Thank you.

That is the end of Section 3. You will have half a minute to check your answers (pause for 30 seconds).

Now turn to Section 4.

Section 4

You will hear a talk by a College Principal. First you have some time to look at questions 31 to 40. (pause for 45seconds)

Now listen carefully to the talk and answer questions 31 to 40.

Well, perhaps I can start this evening by welcoming you all to the College this evening. Some of you, of course, I know well already, but the parents are mostly unfamiliar to me. We are very proud to have you here

Q 31

tonight <u>to present the awards for this year's students,</u> but also to celebrate our centenary, and to celebrate the achievements of the college over that time.

Before we go on to the main business of tonight, the achievement awards, I should like to say a few words to remind you why this College has such a unique reputation in this country. Because it is well-known for what it is, which is quite simply the best engineering institute in the United Kingdom. This is not just my opinion, which might well be biased. It is based on government figures which consistently show that year

after year, we provide <u>the highest levels of education,</u> Q 32 <u>engineering research and pastoral care</u> in the UK.

As most of you know, this is the college's centenary year, and it is important I feel to reflect on the origins of the college. A hundred years ago, the traditional industries of this area – <u>weaving, cutlery</u> <u>making and agriculture</u> – were in sharp decline, and Q 33 when they went, in came that scourge <u>of the past</u>, unemployment and poverty. Our College was founded in order to provide <u>for the some of the</u> <u>poorest but brightest boys</u> of the town and Q 34 surrounding area a way out of the poverty of the time. It was an immediate success, thanks in no small part to the first generation of teaching staff, including Frank Harris, a future president of the Aeronautic Society, and Dr Bart Halliday, whose name is <u>surely</u> <u>known to you all</u> as a Nobel Prize laureate and major Q 35 contributor to the creation of the first atomic bomb. By 1917 the college was turning out <u>300</u> highly skilled, highly qualified <u>graduate engineers</u> a year. Q 36 Former students at this time include Frederick Cantor, who became a researcher at the atomic research station in Minnesota in America, and the painter Lucian Dewdley, RA, who famously didn't complete his studies <u>because of illness.</u> Q 37

After the end of hostilities in 1918, the college was formally attached to the Northern University in Colton, and has remained a part of that institution ever since. The achievements of the graduates and staff of the college in the years since then are too numerous to list here, but I must mention the invention of the <u>Bell racing engine</u>, which has been Q 38 such a powerful force in automotive engineering. These days, the focus of our research has changed to keep pace with the changes in modern technology and while many of you will know that we are particularly well known for our expertise in <u>bridge</u> <u>building technology</u>, you may be surprised to hear Q 39 that none of us has ever actually built a bridge in our lives. These days, it is all done by computer models. So when we worked on the changes ot the Millennium Bridge over the Thames, which wobbled so badly, the first we saw of the bridge was when we walked on it after the completion of the changes. <u>In</u> <u>the dozen or so years that</u> I've been Principal, that is Q 40 probably one of my most fulfilling moments. To be able to undertake this work through theoretical modeling rather than trial and error is surely the goal of engineering research.

That is the end of Section 4. You will have half a minute to check your answers. (pause for 30 seconds)

That is the end of the Listening Test.

You now have 10 minutes to transfer your answers to the Listening answer sheet. (pause 10 minutes)

Please stop writing.

Listening

1 D
2 C
3 C
4 The park/MacGowan Fields
5 the town centre
6 fighting and robberies/muggings
7 A or E
8 E or A
9 A or D
10 D or A
11 A ⎫
12 C ⎬ in any order
13 E ⎭
14 to buy books/for extra cash
15 four/4
16 20/twenty
17 none
18 History of Science
19 Dr Clare
20 French
21 A
22 B
23 C
24 C
25 A
26 homesick/homesickness
27 England
28 in his/own country
29 (friends in) Germany
30 tomorrow
31 of nutrition
32 a healthy diet
33 cure colds/flu
34 in the dark
35 make you intelligent
36 fight/fight off
37 strong teeth
38 10 - 12 mg
39 red blood cells
40 fruit and vegetables

Academic Reading

1 False
2 False
3 True
4 Not Given
5 Not Given
6 False
7 True
8 many problems
9 global warming
10 governmental willingness
11 for many years
12 internationally
13 go away overnight
14 D
15 G
16 B
17 B
18 A
19 C
20 A
21 C
22 B
23 B
24 C
25 C
26 D
27 B
28 A & E
29 C & E
30 B & C
31 B
32 D
33 C
34 A
35 C
36 E
37 British colony
38 find peace
39 legal
40 resource

Listening

1 B
2 C
3 B or E
4 E or B
5 hot and sunny
6 stands
7 beer and wine
8 New Orleans
9 Classical Music/Favourites
10 Ireland
11 Michael
12 Chalvey
13 23rd February 1967
14 Works Yard
15 0912 79509
16 £18,000
17 £450
18 (a) clothes shop
19 none/no
20 £250
21 4/four
22 5/five
23 25/twenty-five
24 Women's
25 Finance
26 C
27 B
28 D
29 B
30 A
31 C or D
32 D or C
33 French and German/French and Greek/German and Greek
34 changing
35 each other's languages
36 a full language
37 (French) New Orleans
38 China and India/China, the Pacific/India, the Pacific
39 than one meaning
40 language recognised

Academic Reading

1 decline
2 fraction
3 vulnerable
4 trapped
5 protection
6 ignored
7 improvements
8 predators
9 No
10 Not Given
11 Yes
12 No
13 No
14 Yes
15 Not Given
16 reservoir
17 (water) (inlet) pipe
18 (water) (Francis) turbine
19 dam (wall)
20 Pelton turbine
21 Cross Flow turbine
22 less efficient
23 is lost
24 forced through pipes
25 high start-up costs
26 E
27 F
28 B
29 G
30 C
31 D
32 H
33 South-Western France
34 bartered objects
35 ideas/concepts
36 symbols
37 sound
38 C
39 D
40 C

	Listening			Academic Reading
1	pasta and salad/pasta/salad		1	ii
2	11.30 - 2.30		2	i
3	£1.50		3	vi
4	50/fifty		4	viii
5	£1.15		5	iii
6	Theatre		6	usually
7	toasted		7	alternately
8	Thursday		8	occasionally
9	1 o'clock/1 p.m.		9	bigger
10	the Main Refectory		10	rotate
11	milkman		11	block
12	broken mirror		12	still
13	general rubbish		13	decrease
14	charity container		14	prone to drought
15	(car/old) batteries		15	about one in six
16	paper		16	less than half
17	magazines		17	about a third
18	by a code		18	one in five
19	offer/give advice		19	tenfold
20	paper industry		20	25%
21	B		21	double
22	A		22	NG
23	D		23	No
24	B		24	NG
25	a badge		25	Yes
26	Arabic		26	Yes
27	the autumn		27	C
28	B		28	B
29	D		29	D
30	C		30	E
31	South Pacific History		31	A
32	Dr. Smith		32	D
33	lecture		33	D
34	4		34	D
35	4		35	D
36	3		36	B
37	2		37	B
38	3		38	B
39	B or E		39	C
40	E or B		40	C

Listening

1 Smith
2 Six/6
3 tour of London/sites
4 6.30 (pm)
5 eat/drink/eat and drink
6 Paris
7 King George
8 8 (pm)
9 because of elections/blocked off roads
10 Van Gogh (accept Goph/Goff) exhibition
11 handouts
12 costing
13 experience
14 smaller companies
15 two
16 having (minor) surgery/in hospital
17 Debbie and Andrew
18 Thursday
19 B
20 D
21 Gina
22 father (in London)
23 Thursday afternoon/2 o'clock
24 Yes
25 for two summers
26 Master's (course)
27 Italian media
28 money
29 (her) college (accommodation)
30 couple of weeks/two weeks
31 D
32 A
33 weaving and cutlery/agriculture and cutlery/weaving and agriculture
34 the poorest boys/the brightest boys
35 famous/known
36 300 graduates/graduate engineers
37 because of illness
38 (Bell) racing engine
39 bridge building (technology)
40 12 years/a dozen years

Academic Reading

1 C
2 B
3 E
4 A
5 E
6 D
7 C
8 E
9 contentious
10 social interaction
11 location
12 advanced scanning equipment
13 defined
14 No
15 Yes
16 Yes
17 No
18 Yes
19 No
20 Yes
21 Not Given
22 Sporozoites
23 Merozoites
24 blood
25 Gametocytes
26 resistance
27 Zygotes
28 viii
29 ix
30 iii
31 iv
32 i
33 vii
34 D
35 A
36 D
37 B
38 B
39 C
40 B

Practice Test 1

1 N
2 N
3 NG
4 N
5 Y
6 Y
7 in advance
8 Miss Smith
9 Mr Jones
10 (practice) fire drill
11 before 10 am
12 room 06
13 room 21
14 ix
15 viii
16 vi
17 ii
18 iv
19 vii
20 specialises
21 encourages
22 routes
23 with
24 recommended
25 money
26 might
27 over $7 million
28 about $325,000
29 about $1 million
30 about $140,000
31 G
32 G
33 L
34 G
35 NG
36 the local economy
37 equally
38 cut/reduced
39 policing/clearing up
40 bars and clubs

Practice Test 2

1 F
2 C
3 B
4 E
5 C
6 D
7 Marilyn
8 History
9 29
10 Susan Heyhoe Hall
11 Danver House
12 Yes
13 Yes
14 Mandy
15 False
16 True
17 True
18 Not Given
19 False
20 False
21 Not Given
22 False
23 to raise money
24 to study (properly)
25 worth the money
26 teaching institutions/teachers
27 a best seller
28 iv
29 vii
30 vi
31 x
32 ix
33 ii
34 iii
35 C
36 D
37 B
38 B
39 B
40 A

MODEL COMPOSITIONS

In both the Academic and General modules the candidate is required to write two essays in one hour. Task One should be a minimum of 150 words and Task Two should be at least 250 words. The student is advised to spend no more than 20 minutes on Task One, leaving 40 minutes for Task Two. Both essays are marked in whole points and more weighting is given to Task Two.

In the Academic module, Task One requires the candidate to study a diagram or table and then to reproduce the information in written form in their own words. Task Two is a discursive essay in which the candidate must write their opinion on a subject or present a balanced argument.

In the General Training module Task One is a letter asking for information or explaining a situation based on a given problem while in Task Two the candidate is given a problem or point of view and must write a solution or justify their opinion.

Below are some specimen essays based on the tasks given in the practice tests. These are examples to show how the essays could be written but other ways of dealing with the questions are also possible. In addition three essays written by students have been graded with the examiner's comments.

Practice Test 1

Writing Task 1

Specimen answer

The graph shows figures for the number of cases of certain diseases in childhood over a period of 50 years from 1950 to 2000. It seems that overall these diseases decreased substantially until about 1980 but then started to increase again.

However, certain diseases have shown different trends. Firstly, malaria appears to have remained fairly constant over the period with between 2 and 3 million cases apart from 1960 when there were only one million instances of the disease in childhood. Also, the figures for some diseases have fallen significantly. Although there were 3 million recorded cases of childhood smallpox in 1950, the disease appears to have been completely eradicated by 1980. In 1950 the number of occurrences of tuberculosis peaked at 6 million and subsequently decreased dramatically until they reached an all time low of 500,000 in 1980. Since then there has been a gradual increase with one million cases in 2000. Finally, the figures for AIDS, which were first recorded in 1980, have shot up from approximately 500,000 and topped 9 million in 2000.

Writing Task 2

Specimen answer

The essay title proposes that younger people are to be preferred as employees because they are more able to accept changes in the workplace compared to a more mature workforce.

One argument in favour of younger employees is that older workers are more often set in their ways and are believed to be resistant to change. There may be an element of truth in this but there are many intelligent and flexible older workers as well as narrow-minded and younger ones set in their ways. Attitude to change is a matter of personality type rather than age. Nonetheless, there are physical changes which progress with age that may make some jobs better suited to a younger element. For example, it seems to be accepted by psychologists that memory diminishes with age. In some modern, hi-tech industries like computer programming, where there is a premium on the regular memorising of large amounts of new information, it would seem younger workers have an advantage.

However, older workers do have many other positive qualities which they can bring to their company working environment. Generally speaking they have more working experience than youngsters and this can benefit the firm whilst planning long-term policies. Their maturity and managerial skills can be viewed as a way of training the younger workers to be leaders themselves.

In conclusion, therefore, it would seem that the proposal in the title has to be rejected since in most work situations a mixture of the best qualities of young and old is to be preferred in order to foster the most productive environment.

Examiner's comments

The content of the writing is understandable, but the reader must make an effort. Many phrases or sentences are difficult to follow. The writer has introduced few relevant facts. The information is poorly organised. There is not much evidence of any linking, either of sentences or of ideas. Vocabulary is impoverished, with an over-reliance on 'get'. Many sentences contain basic grammatical errors such as incorrect irregular verb forms. Punctuation is frequently incorrect and the article is used inappropriately. There is no attempt to use the language of comparison and the essay appears as merely a list of facts based on the bar chart. This candidate would not be able to cope with the demands of a university course.

Grade: **4**

There were many changes in childhood diseases over time in a developing country from 1950 to 2000. The following graphs will identify and discuss trends in the accompanying graph.

In 1950 there were more than 12,000,000 have getten diseases. More than 60% children get the Tuberculosis. 2,000,000 children get the Smallpox, and there were 200,000 children got the Malaria. From 1950 to 1980 the number of children got the Tuberculosis has reduced. it's almost 500.000 children. But the Smallpox has never happened. The number of the Malaria didn't change. The total number of ill children has reduced. In 1980 the world had a new disease - AIDS. From 1980 to 2000. the number of AIDS has increased very quickly. More than 50% children got this disease. it's very difficult for people to reduce this number. The Malaria didn't change from 1950 to 2000. The Tuberculosis began to increase again. The total of the diseases children increased again.

Practice Test 2

Writing Task 1

Specimen answer

This report describes the enrolments for a number of different subjects in universities in the UK, Australia and France.

As can be seen in the table, medicine is the most popular subject studied in Australia with 10% of the total students compared to France and the UK with 6% and 4% respectively. In contrast to this, Australian students in literature number only 1% whereas in the UK it secured 12% of the student

population, the second most favoured branch of learning after media studies which had 15%. Engineering is easily the most studied subject in France with 18% but in Australia and the UK few students selected this as their specialisation with only 3% and 1% respectively. Whilst more modern disciplines such as media studies and sports studies attracted interest in the UK and Australia, gaining 12% and 8% for the latter subject, in France they appear not to exist at all. In all three countries languages do not appear to be very popular with France having the highest numbers at 6% and falling to 2% and 1% for Australia and the UK.

Writing Task 2

Specimen answer

Many of the poorest countries in the world are locked into a cycle of debt to the rich counties. Loans arranged years or even decades ago when interest rates were low, are now very expensive as interest rates are high. What little these countries can earn in foreign exchange through the sale of raw materials, is used to pay off these massive debts.

There are obvious reasons why these debts should be eliminated or reduced. In poor countries it would seem much more sensible to spend foreign currency on medicines to combat disease, machinery to help indigenous industry and agriculture so everyone can work, or on teacher trainers so the education system can combat ignorance and poverty. In the absence of these things Third World citizens are suffering and dying young and those benefiting from the huge interest paid by the underdeveloped countries are the rich bankers in the West. It would be more sensible to reduce these debts and improve the lives of people in the Third World.

It can be argued that these debts should be retained. One argument is that these debts have been legally incurred and like any other debt must be honoured. It would damage the whole banking system if the West decided to abandon some debts and not others. Everyone with a debt would want it eliminated and difficult decisions would have to be made concerning which debts to drop.

Where people are suffering and dying for debts incurred by others sometimes years before they were born, such arguments do not seem logical or powerful. Banks can and do write off bad debts and for humanitarian reasons they should do so for the underdeveloped countries of the Third World.

Practice Test 3

Writing Task 1

Specimen answer

This report describes the number of court appearances for boys and girls between the ages of 10 and 18, in New South Wales, Australia in 1994 and 1995.

As can be seen from the table, at the age of 10 the court appearances for boys are relatively few numbering a mere 25. Until the age of 17 the figures increase steadily every year when they reach a peak at 3495. At 18, the first year of adulthood, there is a dramatic fall in the total male court attendances to 1203 cases.

The trend for girls is similar in as much as the fewest court cases is 4 at the age of 11 and the figures rise steadily until the age of 15 at 530. Between 16 and 17 the figures remained stable at 586 and 596 respectively. At 18, as in the case with the male statistics, the numbers drop significantly to 163.

Although the general trend is similar for both sexes, the court appearances for boys are between three and seven times more frequent than those for girls.

Writing Task 2

Specimen answer

Tourism, it is suggested, is like colonialism in that tourists damage the places they visit and distort the economy. There are a number of presumptions here, that colonialism was bad, that it and tourism distort the local economies and that this distortion is bad. All of these presumptions can be challenged.

Colonialism does not have to be all bad. The Roman colonisation of Britain, for example, brought peace, roads, proper sewerage systems and underfloor heating. It might be argued that these were and are rather good things, and when the Romans left so too did many of these benefits.

However, tourism, or colonialism does not necessarily distort local economies. Where the indigenous industry has dramatically declined, as with coal mining in South Wales, turning a mine into a tourist attraction can be a way of preserving the local economy and the local community by providing regular employment.

It should be noted that the changes tourists bring are not all bad. The money from tourists at Big Pit in South Wales, to continue the example from the previous paragraph, has been

used to improve the local countryside not damage it. In many countries what we see as ugly modern hotels in beautiful locations, are beautiful hotels in beautiful locations to the local population. Modernity is not disliked everywhere, and the jobs and the wealth these things bring are worth far more than the local scenery to people who were previously economically impoverished.

In conclusion, there are obviously advantages and disadvantages to tourism but I believe that the benefits outweigh the drawbacks.

Examiner's comments

The writer clearly has strong ideas on the subject, and these are usually quite fluently expressed, so there is rarely any misunderstanding of the meaning. Despite the lack of formal organising devices such as paragraphing, the ideas are developed logically. There are errors in vocabulary and grammar, but these do not seriously impede understanding. In general, the vocabulary is sufficient to express the writer's meanings. Good use of linking devices.
Grade: **6**

It is claimed that tourism is a modern form of colonialism. It is reported that tourism distorts local economies, causes environmental damage and ruins the places it exploits. However, it is not true at all. So-called "tourism" means a kind of desire to travel around the world, including sceny-viewing and expressing local life. There are many obvious differences between colonialism and tourism. The colonialism has a bad effect on local economies and environment. In my opinion, tourism is good for local economies and environments. In the first place tourism can bring local government much money. Nowadays in lots of regions, tour is the most important income source. Specially many places where the scenies are brilliant are poor areas. In the second place, to solve the local energy problems and starve situation, local governments normally overuse local natural sources. But if tour can make local people rich, local sources will survive. Therefore, tour is good for local environment too. There are many cases to point out that local people benefit great from tourists. In addition, tour will make local people know much other civilisation at the same time, tour will bring other civilisation back their own regions. in a word, tour will boom all kinds of culture instead of ruining them. in conclusion, in contrast with colonialism, tourism brings local people much money and culture. With the development of tourism the local economies and environment will be better and better.

Practice Test 4

Writing Task 1

Specimen answer

This report describes the sales of hardback and paperback books bought in New York from 1960 to 1990 and the types of books which are preferred.

According to the graph, the numbers of both kinds of books have risen with paperback sales being the greater. 20 paperbacks per person were bought in 1960 but by 1985 this figure had more than doubled to 43 books. Concerning hardbacks, the average number bought in 1960 was only two but sales increased steadily until 1985 when those purchased had increased fourfold to eight per person per year.

As can be seen in the histogram, books on self-help were the most popular in 1990 at 28 per person and these have experienced a dramatic increase in popularity since 1960 when only 2 per person were purchased. The most well liked books in 1960 were about religion and politics but they have gradually fallen from 24 and 22 to 16 and 12 respectively in 1990, with only religious books showing a sudden surge in popularity in 1975 when 22 books were sold. The least popular books have always been those on biography and history, peaking in 1960 at 17 and 8 but from 1970 onwards neither book has sold more than 5 copies per person per year.

Writing Task 2

Specimen answer

Many sports, like rugby and football, involve violent contact between players and often lead to injury. Other sports, boxing and wrestling in particular, have the deliberate intention of hurting an opponent. Whether this is acceptable in modern society when at all other times we try to train people not to be aggressive and not to deliberately hurt other people is a debatable point.

The arguments against sports like boxing come from a minority of people who find violence, even in a controlled and institutionalised form, highly disturbing. Their line of reasoning appears to be that it is better for everyone if we live in a violence free society. In order for us, especially children, to learn to avoid such behaviour then it is preferable if we never see it and cannot copy it. If society actually sanctions brutality, as in boxing, it cannot be argued that violence is always unacceptable.

On the other hand, realists point out that cruelty is inherent in society and banning boxing will not alter this. On the contrary, by institutionalising and controlling violence in boxing clubs can help change this. Boys, who would otherwise be part of street gangs outside the law, can be taught to be part of a group and direct their energies at activities which are inside the law. In this environment they can be trained to be better members of society. Organised boxing matches follow elaborate rules and medical facilities are always on hand so, barring accident, no-one should be seriously hurt. How much better this is than uncontrolled street fighting outside the law.

To sum up, it seems to me that there is little to be gained and much to be lost by banning sports such as boxing. Prohibiting boxing will not stop violence in society but it will drive organised fighting outside the law and into the hands of criminals. We would all lose if that occurred.

Examiner's comments

There is a clear logical development in the answer, and the line of argument is quite easy to follow. However, the second paragraph breaks down slightly with a loss of understanding. The tone of the essay is too informal, almost conversational. In general, the vocabulary, despite some weakness in spelling and word-formation, is adequate to the task. There are some grammatical and stylistic oddities which appear to be linked to the writer's first language.
Grade: **7**

On the one hand I agree with that statement, because sports like boxing or wrestling cause aggressive feelings. Especially for young people, which is proved by many scientists. A statistic in the "Oberbadischen" a german newspaper just showed, two weeks ago, that most young people (ruffly about 60% of the viewers) are under the age of 20. So what happens is that young people watch these programms and try to be like the boxers or wrestlers have a fight and have to be in hospital.

So according to this fact boxing and wrestling should be banned and for example, rugby not. Rugby is as tough as boxing.

And after a rugby match shown on TV there are more fights between the fan clubs than after a boxing match. The thing is boxing is not as popular as rugby and so while I disagree with the statement I think rugby is as violent as boxing. But the actual point is that rugby is accepted as a teamsport and accepted in society while boxing isn't. So actually we should ban these kinds of sports as well if you want to prevent society from violent sports.

So in my opinion this statement is totally rubbish because you can't say I want to forbid boxing because it is violent but keep on sending other kinds of violent sports just because they are accepted in society.

General Training Writing

Practice Test 1

Writing Task 1

Specimen answer

Dear Sir/Madam

I wrote to your school last month asking for a brochure and for details of how to arrange accommodation. I have now been waiting for five weeks for a reply but I have received nothing yet. On Tuesday of last week I telephoned your school at 10 o'clock in the morning but I was only able to speak to the caretaker.

I would be very grateful if you would send me your brochure with an application form so I can apply to take an intensive English language summer course in July or August. I would also be grateful for information about the living accommodation you arrange and an application form for this too. I would like to stay with a family to improve my English. As I am vegetarian and a smoker, I would need a family which could accommodate these habits.

I look forward to hearing from you in the near future.

Yours faithfully

Beatrice Ligorio

Writing Task 2

Specimen answer

It is now accepted by most people and governments that the world is experiencing climatic changes and that now and in the future we can expect temperatures to rise. Even when the causes of these changes are known, often very little is done to reverse their effects.

Global warming is the result of industrialisation and our modern way of life. All the things which make modern life easier and more enjoyable seem to cause pollution. The factories we work in, the cars and aircraft we travel in, the air conditioning and central heating we use in the home, all create carbon dioxide and greenhouse gases. At the same time these processes and activities seem to destroy aspects of the ecosystem which might counter this process and keep the system in balance. Thus we destroy and burn or build over the forests and agricultural land which might reabsorb the carbon dioxide.

Dealing with the problem is not a straight forward matter. It is not easy for any government or any person to turn back the clock on the industrial revolution. The prospect of returning to poverty, hard manual labour, disease and early death – the situation which existed before the industrial revolution and which still exists in many non-industrialised countries – is not attractive. Somehow, the governments of the world must coordinate policies which make it possible and attractive for us to use energy efficient means of travel such as walking or the bicycle. We need far more research into truly sustainable sources of energy such as wind and wave power rather than using fossil fuels which release so much carbon dioxide.

In conclusion, as we are aware of the causes of global warning, we must continue to find solutions to the problem otherwise the earth may never recover from its harmful effects.

Practice Test 2

Writing Task 1

Specimen answer

Dear Sir or Madam

I am writing to complain about the quality of some Crunchy Flakes breakfast cereal I bought at the Highgate branch of your supermarket on Tuesday, December 19th.

When we opened the box the following morning in order to have our breakfast, we found the cereal was no longer crunchy but was soggy and covered in blue-green mould. It was clearly inedible. On closer inspection we found that the sell by date on the side of the packet was 5th April 1994. The packet must have been on your shelves for seven years.

I would like to know why your store is selling goods which are clearly dangerous to the public. I would like a replacement packet of cereal, as well as £50 in compensation for the inconvenience and distress you have caused my family. This is not the kind of behaviour I would expect from a supermarket which has such a good repetition in the community.

I look forward to hearing from you.

Yours faithfully

Gunter Mueller

Writing Task 2

Specimen answer

Schools have been with us for many hundreds of years but the school uniform debate is a more recent phenomenon. It probably dates from the development of universal education towards the end of the last century. State schools without uniforms would have contrasted noticeably with the uniformed public schools. Uniforms must have been adopted initially where ambitious state schools sought to demonstrate, through coloured caps, and blazers, that they were as good as the elite public schools.

By the middle of this century, school uniforms became universal in British schools and there were many good reasons why they were retained. They gave a sense of identity to the school. The school is a small society in its own right and one of the tasks of schools was to fit their pupils for society. A uniform is a clear outward manifestation of belonging. There were other benefits too. Where pupils were drawn from a wide cross-section of society a uniform could disguise these differences and paper over divisions within a school. It was a form of social equalisation as well as control. At a time when truancy was more closely monitored, a uniform made pupils out of school at the wrong time much easier to identify.

Whatever the advantages of uniforms, they also had their drawbacks. They were often expensive and something that was intended to be socially integrative could be divisive. They were often unattractive and old-fashioned and could be impractical. During the 1960's it was also felt that uniforms did not fit with the then fashionable ideas on education. This was a time of individuality and self-expression and it began to be thought that education should enable pupils to express and fulfil their own individuality. Wearing a uniform created the opposite effect.

To my mind school uniforms should be retained in all circumstances. They can be modernised and changed according to circumstances but a uniform fulfils one critical aspect of education. It signals to pupils that it is their job to fit into society and not the other way around. If pupils learn nothing else while at school then their time will not have been totally wasted.

SPEAKING
SUGGESTED ANSWERS

The speaking section is divided into 3 sections. It lasts between 11 and 14 minutes with individual candidates being interviewed by one oral examiner.

Part One is a general conversation on familiar topics while Part Two requires the candidate to talk on a particular subject which he has been given time to prepare. The candidate speaks for one or two minutes and the examiner will ask two or three questions at the end of the talk. Part Three is a discussion on more abstract topics which are connected to the subject matter of the student's talk in Part Two. This section of the examination lasts between 4 and 5 minutes.

In the Speaking component the candidate is assessed on his skills in communicating in English and is graded according to his abilities in fluency, vocabulary, grammatical range and accuracy and pronunciation.

Two samples of the Speaking test based on the questions in practice tests one and two are given below. The students in these tests could gain maximum scores depending on their pronunciation skills.

Candidates should be aware that it is standard procedure for the oral interviews to be recorded on cassette and that this section is marked in whole points only.

Practice Test 1

I'd like you to tell me something about yourself.

Is your family large or small?
We are only a small family. Myself and two sisters.

What do other members of your family do?
Maria, my eldest sister, has a weekend job working in a paper shop but Anastasia doesn't work. She's too young. My father works, of course, he is a manager in a cotton factory in Larissa. My mother doesn't work now although she used to be a teacher.

When was the last time all your family were together? What did you do?
We were together at Easter. We did what we Greeks usually do at Easter which is to roast a whole lamb on a spit on Easter Day. Then we shared it with all our friends in the village. It was lovely. We really enjoyed it.

What do you do as a family on special occasions like weddings or feasts?
Easter is the main feast where we do something special. For weddings we dress in our best formal clothes for the wedding ceremony. There's a tradition I don't think you have in Britain where after the priest declares the couple married, he leads them around the altar 3 times and everybody throws rice and rose petals over the couple. It's very good fun. Then we go to a reception and have a meal.

Is there a member of your family you are especially close to?
I'm very close to my sister Maria.

Why?
We grew up together. We've always gone to school together and done everything together. If I do go to study in Britain, I'll miss her dreadfully.

I'm going to give you a subject to talk about. You have to talk about if for about two minutes. Before you start talking I'll give you about one minute to think and to write down some notes. Do you understand what you are going to do?

Yes, that's fine.

Here's a pen and some paper to write on.

This is your subject. I'd like you to talk about a trip or holiday which you have taken recently.
You only have a short time to speak so I will stop you after a while. Don't worry about that. You can start talking now.
Well, I'd like to talk about the holiday I took last summer with my sister Maria when we went to the island of Corfu. We had never been allowed to go away on holiday without our family before so it was very exciting. We had a room in a hotel in a resort called Ipsos. It was very busy and full of other young people on their holidays. There were lots of bars and restaurants to visit there, and we met a lot of people from Britain and Germany. At first we didn't like it because it was so noisy – the discos are so loud and they continue all night! And it was all so strange and different not having Mum and Dad with us. But then we made some friends and took a bus into Corfu town itself and that was lovely. The buildings are all Italian in style and quite different from Athens where everything is 1960s concrete. It was so pretty. And we visited the church of Saint Spiridon

125

and were allowed to see the body of Saint Spiridon himself. His body is preserved in a special casket and you can see his face and at special times they uncover his feet, which have special slippers on, and you can kiss them and say a special prayer for help. The church was full of small silver gifts from people Saint Spiridon has helped ...

Thank you.

Had you been on a trip like this before?

We've been on holiday to the islands before. We've been to Santorini and to Kos. But, as I said, we'd never been alone before. It was very different being by ourselves like that.

You've been telling me about a trip you've made. I would like to talk to you about some questions related to travel.

Do you think travel broadens the mind?

Oh, yes, I think so. I mean I know that the world is getting smaller and we all watch the same films and TV programmes, but you still meet people who do different things, like different things and speak in different languages from you. And when you meet them and get to like them, you like some of the new things you meet. I think it makes you more tolerant. You know more so you can understand and accept more variety.

Describe how the tourism industry has grown in your country.

It's grown enormously in Greece in the last twenty years. An island like Corfu which had very little industry only 20 years ago is now quite rich. Whole new resorts and villages have grown up on the coast to cater for tourists and they only work during the summer. In a town like Corfu itself the tourists mean that there is good business for restaurants and bars and so on.

Describe what things your area offers tourists.

In Greece we offer tourists guaranteed sun, beautiful beaches and a very relaxed lifestyle. We love children in Greece so for families there is always a lot for them to do and there is no problem taking them to restaurants and so on. Also, Greece has a long history so there are many different historical sites to visit if that's what you want.

Evaluate what type of tourists it brings to your area.

I think it probably brings two main types. Firstly, there are the young people who come for the sun, the sea, and the bars. Then there are the families. They will also like the sun and the sea but will also want the fully catered holidays that modern hotels can provide.

Evaluate how tourism is good for the economy.

Tourism brings in foreign currency. We are an agricultural country, so we don't have industrial products to trade. Tourism must be the most important foreign currency earner in the economy. Hotels and bar owners obviously benefit but so do a lot of other people. The people who work in the hotels, those who run the tourist shops, the restaurant owners all make a good living out of tourism.

Speculate on what other benefits might tourism bring to a country.

We think that the tourist trade has brought us closer to the heart of Europe and made us more European. For a country that is on the edge of Europe this is very important.

How has tourism changed your area/country for the better?

So many people were very poor a generation ago and tourism has changed so many peoples' lives with the money it brings. The larger houses, running water, electricity and cars, there are so many ways we have all benefited.

How has tourism changed your area/country for the worse?

I believe it has damaged the ecology a great deal. Near my village, we used to have seals which would share the beach with the villagers in summer. We had one end and the seals had the other. Now the seals have gone and I guess they will never come back. There are too many people, too much noise, too much rubbish for them to tolerate. It's a great pity.

Discuss whether the tourism trade is a good thing or a bad thing.

There is no simple answer to this question because it is both good and bad, of course. The wealth which tourism brings doesn't just make us personally richer but also provides us with hospitals, better education and so many good things. But there is a price to pay for all this. The lifestyle is changing and so is the environment. I would think that, on balance, tourism is a good thing. But we can do more to make sure that tourism doesn't take away all the things that we love about Greece.

Thank you. The Speaking Test is now finished.

Practice Test 2

I'd like you to tell me something about yourself.

Are you studying, or do you have a job?
I'm a student at the moment.

What exactly are you studying?
I'm taking by bachelor's degree in Economics at the University of Salamanca.

Have you been studying it for a long time?
Yes, we begin studying economics at school when we are about 12. Then I chose to go on and study Economics when I went to university.

Why did you decide to study it?
I was good at Economics at school and I quite enjoyed it, so I didn't mind continuing with it at university. I chose it at university because I want to get a job in the Ministry of Economics and a degree is an essential requirement.

Are you enjoying the course? Why? Why not?
I enjoy some of it. I enjoy the History of Economic Thought much more than the theoretical modelling. I must admit it's rather boring, if I am honest. But you have to study it.

I'm going to give you a subject to talk about. You have to talk about if for about two minutes. Before you start talking I'll give you about one minute to think and to write down some notes. Do you understand what you are going to do?

Yes, that's fine.

Here's a pen and some paper to write on.

This is your subject. I'd like you to talk about a film you have seen recently.
You only have a short time to speak so I will stop you after a while. Don't worry about that. You can start talking now.
I'm going to talk about a film "The Mummy Returns". I'm choosing it because it was the film I saw with some friends last weekend so it's fresh in my mind. It isn't a serious film or anything. It's meant to be light-hearted and funny. It tells the story of an ancient Egyptian priest who is accidentally brought back to life and wants to raise his army from the dead. The army and the priest have supernatural powers and they will be able to rule the world. To raise his army and rule the world the priest needs a special bracelet which will allow him to control the Scorpion King – I didn't really understand that bit. But a small boy, the child of some archaeologists, puts it on. The priest kidnaps the boy and takes him to Egypt and the boy's parents go after him to rescue him and save the world. They travel to an oasis in the

middle of the Egyptian desert and fight lots of supernatural enemies. Then the boy's father fights the priest and saves his son and saves the world. Actually it is more complicated than that but the story isn't really serious. The special effects are very good and there are some funny characters. It isn't really meant to be scary or anything. I enjoyed it because it was funny. The actors were good and the make-up and special effects to show the Mummy coming back to life were excellent.

Thank you.

What kind of films do you enjoy?
I like something that is light, maybe a comedy. I like it to be intelligent, with clever dialogues that give the actors something to work with and show some depth of character. I don't really like violence or war films.

You've been telling me about the films you enjoy. Now I'd like you to talk about the film industry and generally about entertainment.

Which countries do you think make the best films?
Well, Hollywood makes the most successful films and they can be good films too. But often other countries make more interesting films. The French make films which are often more challenging and intellectual and require better acting. I like French films a lot.

What do you think makes a good film?
I like it to have a good script that allows the characters to develop as real, believable people. I like an interesting topic, something that makes you think or challenges the way you think about things. And I like to see actors bringing the characters to life and making them convincing. Too often Hollywood films are formulaic. The characters are flat and lifeless and there is no interest or novelty in the story.

Evaluate the influence of violence in films on young people.
I think young people take a lot of their ideas from films and film stars. They copy the way they dress and speak. So I suppose it would be strange if they didn't copy the violence they see, too. I think young people are more violent now and they tolerate violence more. I don't like it myself.

Compare films from your country with Hollywood films.
I guess Hollywood would be concerned with big commercial blockbusters, rather than art. I think they can be very inward-looking for films intended to be seen worldwide. They don't always interest us in Spain. But Spanish films often deal with topics that are much more of interest to Spain. That's nice.

Compare modern music and the traditional music in your country.

Well, of course in Spain the traditional music is flamenco in the south, with dancers and guitarists. It is gypsy music. It is popular now in a different form – do you know the Gypsy Kings? But mainly popular music is liked by the younger generation. It's electric, whereas traditional music is acoustic, and it's better suited to small places like tavernas and dance halls.

Tell me how music can bring people together.

I think you can see this at parties and weddings. Everybody likes to dance to the traditional songs whether they are old or young. But even at these gatherings when they play modern music you can see a generation gap. The old people sit at their tables and talk while the young people dance. I think that is sad.

Describe the most popular musicians/forms of music in your country.

That is difficult. Flamenco is still very popular and someone like Joachim Cortes is very popular in Spain and everywhere. He's very flamboyant and combines traditional flamenco music and dance with more modern ballet moves. It's more like art. People like that.

Thank you. The Speaking Test is now finished.